To my granddaughter, the nicest addition to the tribe.

WE ARE MANY, WE ARE ONE: NEO-TRIBES AND TRIBAL ANALYTICS IN 21ST CENTURY AMERICA

©2016 John Zogby

TABLE OF CONTENTS

INTRODUCTION

"You are what you eat", at least according to a now well-worn cliché. But even if that had been true once, it's not any more. "You are what you choose to be and who you choose to be associated with", I say. And what you are is no longer as easily defined as it used to be. Ethnicity has always been a powerful determinant of values and behaviors, but so many of us Americans are multi-ethnic and multi-racial. The United States has distinct regions and regional differences still standout. But we are more and more mobile thus many southerners have moved north as many northerners and Midwesterners have relocated south. And many millions of people have moved west. Immigration is a huge force beyond its numbers. Big and small cities now have a polyglot of different groups from Latin America, the Middle East, Asia, and Eastern Europe. Millennials have gone to school with diverse peoples, date and marry multi ethnically, and are foodies who eat all sorts of unique and fused foods. Millennials themselves are diverse racially and ethnically.

So who are you, anymore? Your heritage may be Dutch but you are a seventh generation American with an Italian surname and have never set foot in Amsterdam or Florence. You may be Jewish but haven't been inside a synagogue in decades. Some folks may define you as "suburban" but you work and play in the big city, and you may just move back there. Your zip code reveals that Wal-Mart is very popular and there is a high preponderance of subscribers to *Field and Stream* but you shop online at Bloomingdales and prefer *Vanity Fair.*

Add to the mix global mobility, telecommunications, and vast social networks, and Americans cannot be so easily pigeonholed into neat one-dimensional categories. So old identifiers no longer work to pinpoint who people are.

The story of the Neo-Tribes and Tribal Analytics is one of process, content, and collaboration. Professional market researchers and social scientists have developed numerous ways over the years to package people into clusters of common features in order to best understand who they are, how they behave, what interests them and what makes them tick. Mainly, these forms of "segmentation" and "cluster analysis" of populations have been based on demographics or common regional culture, but have ignored or downplayed shared behaviors and outlooks and thus have become outmoded, obsolete, and even useless in a world where changes can be dramatic and momentary. In addition, they have been cumbersome (large samples derived by telephone surveys) and expensive. On top of that, they were inflexible – what you got had to have a shelf-life of several years because it was hard to justify the cost and time. But what can possibly have a long shelf–life in today's world?

The uniqueness of Tribal Analytics is that it 'segments' the population based on self-identified tribal affinities — shared values, life philosophies and outlooks. In doing so, it transcends demographics and other category-specific attitudes and behaviors that would be the basis of a traditional market segmentation study.

"Because of this", according to Dayna Dion, communications strategist and former Cultural Strategy Director for Ogilvy & Mather in Chicago, "Tribal Analytics is a critical tool for the emerging practice of cross-cultural marketing, which just recently took root." (The Cross-Cultural Marketing and Communications Association was established in 2013.)

Demographics are always interesting as a way of understanding and predicting behavior and response, but they too are limiting and incapable of understanding the diversity within age, regional, income, ethnic groups. For example, the Greatest Generation included, at one and the same time, both arch-conservative William F. Buckley and militantly antiwar radical David Dellinger. Who is the proto-typical Millennial: Chelsea Clinton or Lindsey Lohan? Josh Groben or LeBron James? Demographics are just simply too broad. Census tracts and zip codes served their purpose for many decades as a key to understanding people in geographical context, but just what role does geography play today in a world of mobility and mobile technology that offers global information and connection to people? "Microtrends", developed by the great pollster Mark Penn, are fun and, I must admit, thought-provoking, but are they something that marketers or management can really use? The work of Joel Garreau (*The Nine Nations of North America*), Dante Chinni (*Our Patchwork Nation*), and Colin Woodard (*American Nations*) are all fascinating and based on placing people into a broad cultural context that makes sense. These books have been very illuminating – and are never far from my reach -- but they still miss the boat when it comes to understanding communities of interest that motivate people and drive their decisions. Garreau's work was pathbreaking because it focused on culture and transcended traditional political boundaries. Thus, why shouldn't Maine and northern New England be joined together with French-speaking Canadian territories? They shared so much history, ancestry, and religious heritage. Chinni's brilliant "patchwork" has categorized counties by huge amounts of hard data and opinion research – as well as some excellent gumshoe reporting and analysis. But he doesn't account for substantial differences in culture and politics among counties that share common silos. For example, both Luzerne County in Pennsylvania and Oneida County in New York have seen a huge influx of immigrants in the past two decades. But Luzerne is notorious for its efforts to discriminate against and push away these newcomers while Oneida has become world-renowned for welcoming refugees and others. Should we really consider them "sister counties"? Woodard has actually identified eleven "nations" of North America. He blends together shared history, cultural similarities, common ideals and even linguistic similarities. Again, like Garreau and Chinni, he has gone outside the boxes of tradition. But we come away from Woodard's tome with a sense that the "nations" are so different that there is no glue that can possibly hold them together. The "nations" are fascinating but the message is hopeless.

So something is still missing. There is literally a new landscape. We inhabit a world of cyberspace and it is also in our minds and hearts – not in our physical neighborhoods, voting precincts, our Rotary meetings, or our churches and stadiums. **This new world is as much about how we choose to identify ourselves, how we define our own priorities, and who we ourselves choose as our cohort as it is about where we physically work, play or worship.** We researchers very much need a bottom-up process that goes directly to people and allows them to tell their own story first, before we start to re-tell it for them. This was the initial premise that drove what I eventually came to refer as "tribal analytics." The Crosby, Stills and Nash song "Love the One You're

With" can no longer simply refer to your next door neighbor or your last e-Harmony date. Instead, it is who we share our own space with – but "space" means less and less about geography.

Thus those of us in the business of understanding what makes our fellow humans think and act need something new, an attempt to place people in a more fitting context in a world where it matters less where they live, when they were born, where they went to school , and how much they earn. As well, new technologies and sources for data seem to argue for a new process of segmentation -- something less consultant-driven or researcher-driven. Would it be possible to let the subjects of inquiry actually determine their own communities of interest? Just as humans have always found ways to organize themselves into "packs", "tribes", and "villages" – maybe we could find out firsthand from the respondents of our surveys how they cluster themselves?

This is the "era of the non-expert", as Jeff Howe pointed out in *Crowdsourcing* in 2009, and the internet has empowered us to define ourselves and find our own friends. Space and geography are less and less relevant. **It is no longer about where people are born or where they live. It is more about who they are, how they see themselves, and with whom they choose to identify.** Rather than enter this turf with researcher-imposed hypotheses and presumptions, we decided to let the non-experts do the work for themselves.

But in addition to dealing with the declining factors of geography and expert-driven hypotheses, there is also the factor of collecting usable data in real time in a world where time is both of the essence and fleeting. Clusters will change under the same conditions as people do. Is there a research methodology that can produce actionable data and be repeated in an affordable and time-friendly manner?

So I set out with my team (first at Zogby International , then Zogby Analytics) in 2009 to try to develop a unique methodology that could let people tell us who they really think they are and to serve a world that is constantly changing. We employed a multi-stage series of surveys and analytics to derive America's "neo-tribes". Our mission is not only to more accurately represent where Americans categorize themselves to-day and to assist clients in finding, messaging, and delivering products and services to their key tribes – but also, to create a high-speed and flexible methodology that can capture "emerging tribes" and push aside "diminishing tribes". In two important ways Tribal Analytics segmentation is very different:

- It is dynamic and flexible enough to capture changes in patterns of people's lives and priorities
- It is bottom-up, not top-down, in its approach to segmentation in that it is derived solely from survey research with no pre-established hypotheses

Initially, as described above, the process was launched with three separate quantitative online surveys nationwide to test if the idea of tribes made any sense. In each survey we learned from declarative statements made to represent distinctive values and attributes that there were Americans who could clearly be categorized into groups that represented dominant values and worldviews. Importantly, in the Zogby Analytics open-ended surveys, Americans actually got to name their own tribes in addition to identifying the attributes that describe and offer most meaning to their lives. As the tribes formed early in the survey process, and were validated and shaped in subsequent surveys, distinct differences clearly emerged. We also discovered higher correlations with certain types of behaviors. From these tests, we then found through cluster analysis that at times there was a clear pattern of "tribal border crossings" – whereby members of tribes were very distinct from each other but that there were intersections of agreement and other commonalities that allowed communicators to develop crossover messages. On the other hand, there were also patterns of "tribal dissonance", whereby differences were so profound and intense that these could actually resemble warring tribes of old.

So more and more we are what we choose to be, with whom we choose to connect, and how we define our own cohort. And, like the world in which we inhabit, our cohort may not be for a lifetime. Tribes may be forever, for a long time, or ephemeral and fluid just like everything else.

America's new tribes are a rich tapestry, multidimensional, and a kaleidoscope of different identifications. The packages are not so neatly defined either. As we will see, the Happy Hedonists love living and having fun. There are a good number of younger people – but many more go to a place of worship at least weekly than 18-29 year olds do. In fact, these concert-going, tail-gate loving pleasure seekers can be found attending a place of worship almost as frequently as the Bible-thumping God Squad.

CHAPTER 1

WHAT DOES BEING IN A "TRIBE" MEAN?

Tribal membership means a lot of things. Since humans first began to form groups, even initial tribes were based on a shared heritage or extended family network, tests and oaths of loyalty, common enemies, protocols for cooperation, initiation rites and rites of passage into adulthood, and acceptance of rules of behavior. Leadership was hierarchical and tribal membership shared symbols and rituals. As Edward O. Wilson has written in *The Social Conquest of the Earth:*

> *People must have a tribe. It gives them a name in addition to their own and social meaning in a chaotic world. It makes the environment less disorienting and dangerous. The social world of each modern human being is not a single tribe, but rather a system of interlocking tribes, among which it is often difficult to find a single compass. People savor the company of like-minded friends, and they yearn to be in one of the best – a combat marine regiment, perhaps, an elite college, the executive committee of a company, a religious sect, a fraternity, a garden club – any collectivity that can be compared favorably with the other, competing groups of the same category.*

But tribes are not inherited today. Fewer people – especially in the United States -- are born into a sense of permanent structures and, above all, tribes are more fluid and dependent on the response to shared realities and the need to adapt to these shared experiences.

Research in social psychology has shown that group membership is one of the most powerful influences on human behavior. Group membership leads to things as varied as altruism, in-group bias, conformity and holding extreme views. Group members develop social identities which drive social comparisons, self-esteem and stereotyping. And as Pulitzer-prize-winning journalist Tina Rosenberg shows in her book, *Join the Club: How Peer Pressure Can Transform the World,* belonging to small groups provides more than an opportunity to connect with others, it is defining, empowering, self-actualizing, and enhancing.

Tribal membership offers us a boost in our lives. In-group bias is one of the best established findings in social psychology. It describes preferential treatment of those perceived to be members of the same group. Early studies have uncovered just how arbitrary the criterion of group membership can be and still exert a powerful influence on short-term behavior (this is called a "minimal group paradigm").

People are more likely to cooperate with others who share with them trivial similarities such as birthday date. For example, in a study by Downs, Miller and Prentice (1998) individuals were more likely to co-operate in a Prisoner's dilemma (experimental set-up that pits individuals against each other) if they were told (incorrectly) that they share a birthday with the other person. Finch and Cialdini (1989) have shown that perceptions of historical figures are more positive if people believe those figures share a birthday with them.

Groups exert a powerful effect on one's judgment – making one doubt their very basic powers of vision. This was shown in the early studies (1951) by Asch, in an experimental set-up where an individual was placed in a group and asked to compare length of a target line to three other lines and say which of those three lines is most similar in length to the target line. Unbeknownst to the subject, the other seven members of the group colluded to claim the shorter line to be a longer one. In about 30% of cases, individuals succumbed to the group pressure and let it override their own perception of length.

Tribal loyalties can lead to cooperation and sense of belonging. Tribal loyalties can also have devastating effects. Wars are examples of altruism towards one's tribe, but hatred and aggression toward those not in one's tribe. Violating important group norms leads to punishment, even death. Group norms are informed on a more benign level through ridicule and ostracism.

The crucial part for the psychological essence of the tribal bond is that people see it as a bond – the tribal identification has to be something that people either themselves see as relevant or are somehow manipulated (as in social security and other studies) to see as relevant. Just because people can be categorized into groups doesn't make those groups real at the psychological level.

This is especially true of demographic variables. People can be categorized according to many dimensions, such as age, marital status, educational level, household income etc. All women belong to a group, but they must feel as a part of that group in order for group processes to take place; they need to feel as a team; the mere presence of shared characteristics won't do.

Building on experimental results in the minimal group paradigm as well as his own experience of Holocaust, sociologist Henry Tajfel has developed a social identity theory that contains the following insights about the nature of group membership:

- Personal identity', which differentiates the unique self from all other selves, is different from 'social identity', which is the internalization of, often stereotypical, collective identifications. Social identity is sometimes the more salient influence on individual behavior.

- Group membership is meaningful to individuals, conferring social identity and permitting self-evaluation. It is a shared representation of who one is and the appropriate behaviour attached to who one is.

- Comparison and evaluation between groups is generically bound up with the establishment and maintenance of in-group distinctiveness, in an interplay of internal similarity and external difference.

- Groups distinguish themselves from, and discriminate against, other groups in order to promote their own positive social evaluation and collective self-esteem.

- Individuals and groups with unsatisfactory social identity seek to restore or acquire positive identification via mobility, assimilation, creativity or competition.

- Individuals, in using stereotypical categories to define themselves thus, bring into being human collective life.

In other words, self-categorization into a group is a powerful psychological process affecting many facets of one's view of himself and his behavior toward others. It can exert a powerful influence on one's long term and short term behavior and attitudes. However, the crucial element underlying psychological processes of group member is self-categorization – members' own awareness and acceptance of their membership which goes beyond mere shared characteristics.

As we see in this book, the process of self-categorization is an important component of Tribal Analytics and certainly suggests fluidity as personal contexts change. Could the loss of a loved one turn a high-flying Adventurist into a member of the faith-centered God Squad? Does a physician-mandated healthy food-based diet transform an Epicurean-focused Happy Hedonist into a Self-Perfectionist? Will the birth of a first child cause an epiphany in a nihilistic Outsider and render her a Go With the Flow? The process of Tribal Analytics is a dynamic one and can provide answers to questions like these.

Tribal Analytics, the product of seven years of research and development, is a study of how people self-categorize based on self-conceptions: how they perceive themselves as members of a group(s). It sheds light on the social identities most salient in driving attitudes and behaviors. In practical terms, the process involves use of the unique and time-tested screener questions – both forced-choice and open-ended – that allow for the categorization of respondents into tribes. The methodology is such that it can include some or all of the generic tribes Zogby Analytics discusses in these pages, along with new and specific tribes that will fit client needs. Once the tribes are defined, the character- and behavior-types can then be applied to the full nationwide or client base. (A more detailed methodology explanation appears below in the Appendix).

Asch, S.E. (1951). Effects of group pressure on the modification and

distortion of judgments. In H. Guetzkow (Ed.), Groups, leadership and men(pp. 177–190). Pittsburgh, PA: Carnegie Press.

Brewer, M. B., Kramer, R. M. (1986_. Choice behavior in social dilemmas: effects of social identity, group size, and decision framing. J. Pers. Soc. Psychol. 50:543-49

Finch, J. F., & Cialdini, R. B. (1989). Another indirect tactic of (self-) image management: boosting. Personality and Social Psychology Bulletin, 15, 222-32.

Jenkins, Richard (1996). Social identity. Routledge.

Miller, D. T., Downs, J. S., & Prentice, D. A. (1998). Minimal conditions for the creation of a unit relationship: The social bond between birth-daymates. European Journal of Social Psychology, 28, 475-81.

CHAPTER 2

INTRODUCING: AMERICA'S NEO TRIBES

Well, here they are – the 11 Neo-Tribes that have been defined since the beginning of the process in 2009 and have solidified with each phase of our research. Zogby Analytics' super-sample of over 8,013 adult respondents has yielded the following:

1. THE GOD SQUAD – 24.9% OF ADULTS.

The Z-File on the God Squad – Young Senator Barack Obama really stepped into a pile at a 2008 San Francisco fundraiser when he described economically strapped Pennsylvanians as "clinging to their guns and religion". Arrogance aside, he was on to something. Our God Squad is indeed relying on God, family, and traditional values to give them some stability and an explanation for their world gone sour. Unfairly portrayed as extremist and fanatical, these are people who are hurting – lots of people struggling, focused on survival, and hoping for salvation in heaven.

They aim for authenticity and are guided by their faith. Not impressed by frills or the high life, their greatest expectations are for success in the afterlife, not so much here on Earth or today. Modesty and other values that refer back to a kinder, gentler America, community, and family, the God Squad may be at the top of the list of those who sympathize with the Tea Party, except they lack the harder edge, the anger. Less willing to *compromise, they are the bedrock of an older America, but they will not pass from the scene soon – **50% are under 50 years of age.***

The evidence of the role of faith in the lives of members of the God Squad is pervasive. When we asked simple one-word associations that "best describes the meaning of (your) life", a very large percentage of this tribe (49%) identified with "blessed and saved". No other tribe even came close to that high figure. Their second highest descriptive value was "honorable and trustworthy", strongly suggesting that their aim in their lives is to follow a moral imperative consistent with their faith in God.

Together with the Land of the Free, the God Squad is the most conservative of any tribe, including the 35% who say they are "conservative on all issues", not just on federal spending or social issues. Only 12% call themselves liberals – including just 4% all the time (the lowest), 2% on government spending, and 6% on social issues. There are only 23% moderates in the tribe.

THE GOD SQUAD

24.9% OF ADULTS

LIFE MISSION/ MEANING

"To live for and serve God, my faith."

FACTORS IN CHOOSING FELLOW TRIBE MEMBERS

Love of God, faith, authenticity, duty, responsibility.

DEFINITION OF SUCCESS

Happiness, no frills.

ONE THING MISSING TO COMPLETE LIFE

To find a cure for cancer.

STRENGTHENING TRIBAL BONDS

Attending a place of worship, a spiritual retreat, family and school events.

DEMOGRAPHICS

Gender God Squad has the highest ratio of women (60%) to men (40%) of any tribe.

Income They have the second greatest concentration of household earnings under $50,000 (54%) and the second lowest number of households making over $100,000 (15%)

Residence They are tied for the highest percentage who live in a rural area (24%), while about average living in large cities (23%), small cities (20%), and suburbs (33%).

They are among the most likely to own their own home (68%).

Religion The God Squad is most likely to be Protestant (72%) and least likely to be Jewish (1%). By far, the God Squad is most likely to identify as Born Again or Evangelical (79%). Their attendance at weekly (plus) religious services is about double the next highest group (61%).

Family They are the third highest to be married (56%) and have children under 17 living at home (30%). But a lower than average number are single (22%) and they have lower than average numbers of divorced or separated among the tribes (18%).

Race/Ethnicity 68% are white, and while they have the third lowest percentage of Hispanics (8%), they have the highest percentage of African Americans (19%).

Age They are evenly balanced by age (50% are over 50), but 33% are 30-49 and another 17% are 18-29.

Employment The God Squad has the second highest percentage of retirees (19%), while 41% (tied for lowest) are working full or part-time. Only 18% fear losing a job in the next 12 months (on the lower side). About one in ten said they lost a job in the past year due to corporate downsizing (in the middle), one in five work at a job that pays less than a previous job (second lowest), and 15% have gone without food for 24 hours at a time because of a lack of money or food in the past three months.

Lifestyle 63% do not consider themselves to be social networkers, while 37% do (on the low side). They are the second least likely to have an active passport (39%), to be members of the Investor Class (22%) – which includes those adults who tell Zogby Polls that they have some sort of investment portfolio and who "consider themselves to be members of the Investor Class, and tied for least likely to consider themselves to be in the Creative Class (31%) – a term coined by economist Richard Florida, which includes the 40 million Americans who work in the knowledge sector. About 5% admit to being Lesbian/Gay/Bisexual/Transgender – among the lowest of any tribe.

The God Squad shares some important values with other tribes: a majority feels the importance of regular exercise (57%) and eating healthy (69%) but what sets them apart is from whence they get their name – God and faith. Eighty-three percent – by far more than any other tribe and light years ahead of most of the tribes – place special importance on a "place of worship" in their lives. They also rank third among tribes for identifying "the American flag" as most important to them (76%).

POLITICS

At 56%, this tribe is the most likely to say they are conservative on most issues – and are least likely of all the tribes to identify as moderate (29%) or liberal (15%). Thirty four percent – the most of any tribe – say they are sympathetic to the Tea Party. The only 14% who sympathize with Occupy Wall Street is the lowest of the tribes.

They have the second highest percentage who identify as Republican with 43%, while 33% are Democrats, and 24% are independent – both of the latter are the lowest of any tribe.

Their conservatism is clear and across the board. When we asked the God Squad, whose America they preferred, Barack and Michelle Obama's or Ron and Rand Paul's, they chose the Paul's by a factor of 40% to 27%. This margin is second only to the Land of the Free, however 22% selected neither, possibly because we did not offer a more purely social conservative option.

We also posed two statements about government – one which noted that government must be cut but recognizing that government does good things and does employ people vs. the other which stated that presently government spending is unsustainable and Americans are on the road to serfdom. Slightly under one in five (19%) of the God Squad chose the first statement (tied for the lowest) while 71% chose the second (the most of any tribe).

On abortion, three in five (59%) say they were pro-life either in all instances (20%) or except in cases involving rape (39%). That is the greatest support of any tribe. The 14% of the God Squad who said they were pro-choice in all instances were the lowest of any tribe.

Almost two in five say that "following politics" (38%) and their "local government" (39%) are very important to them, which puts them in the same league with fellow conservative leaning tribes like the Land of the Free, the One True Path, and the Dutifuls,

They tell us that they voted overwhelmingly for former Governor Mitt Romney over President Barack Obama in 2012 – 61% to 39%.

 HABITS AND ATTITUDES

If there were only one big box store left to do shopping the God Squad would be at Sears (18%) or Macy's (15%) and Costco (15%). These are both traditional standbys for shoppers with traditional and simple tastes. Sears and Costco are low priced options.

Which store least represents the core values of the God Squad? Simple answer: Neiman-Marcus (25%) and Bloomingdales (17%).

While not registering as high as other tribes in their social responsibilities as consumers, members of the God Squad do care about the sources of the food they consume. Thus, 61% say they follow closely the nutritional data on food labels before purchasing. This percentage does not put them in the same category of concern as the Creators

(77%) the Self-Perfectionists (76%), or the One True Path (71%) but it does indicate that a heightened awareness about and greater demand for transparency in food labeling is not merely the realm of a narrow group of interests.

Under one half of the God Squad (46%) say they follow the environmental safety impact of the contents of the food they purchase , while 50% do not. Again, this figure puts them closer to the bottom on such concerns but clearly they are not dismissive. And 42% say they follow whether their food is composed of "genetically modified organisms" (GMO).

The local or "slow food movement" has caught on like brush fire in the past few years. Importantly, this is not just a hippie/granola/college town phenomenon. Among the very conservative God Squad, 56% look for locally grown food before they make their food purchasing decisions.

They remain by far and away the most devoted to and defined by their faith in and love of God (93%) – 14 points higher than their nearest rival, the One True Path. They are considerably more likely than any other tribe to attend a place of worship at least weekly more than any other tribe (85%) and to find satisfaction attending a spiritual retreat (70%). They seek authenticity and honesty (90%) and are tied for first placing emphasis on simplicity (69%) and family (88%). Importantly, those are the very qualities they look for and ultimately choose in those they want as their tribal members. Three in four (77%) are Born Again or evangelical.

The God Squad is not impressed by material pleasures. Only 7% would spend a $5,000 windfall on themselves, the lowest of any tribe and 38% (the second lowest) said they would feel guilty for spending as little as $50 on themselves – 57% under $100. They are among the least likely to believe that the American Dream is alive and well, least concerned about wanting "to appear of a higher class", and place the lowest important of any tribe on the environmental imprint of what they purchase. To be sure, 19% of this group do fantasize about living in a "Mediterranean villa" ("let God's will be done" – Editor's Note) – but that is the lowest of any tribe. Two in five (the highest) say they would still be living in their current home in a fantasy. One in five of the God Squad – more than any other tribe – feel they could live comfortably on their current income or less. Two in five (39%) could live comfortably on 20% more than their current income or less, again more than any other tribe. They love Wal-Mart not only as their store of choice but also because of the fact that 31% shop there at least every week-- the second highest among the tribes. They are the least inclined toward Target.

The God Squad hates "celebrity gossip" – only 10% say it is very important to them.

Mainly women (60%), they have among the lowest average income of the tribes and have among the highest percentages who are married. They are also more likely to be found in the rural areas than in bigger cities. They are among the lowest in having passports, are the least likely to be working full- or part-time, and 24% say they are working at a job that pays less than a previous job (more than any other tribe). Less than two in three (63%) are white, but 20% are African American (the second highest of any tribe). They also have the lowest percentage of members who have at least some college (32%). They are number one in support of the Tea Party and 56% describe themselves as conservative.

THE GOD SQUAD IN THEIR OWN WORDS

This is not a one dimensional tribe but it truly is God-centered and this is further revealed by the follow up interviews and emails we received. Jasmine from Pasadena, California said that the motto that drives her is "God is good and he wants me to live my life according to His will and desire". Her chief defining moments in life came when "my dad went into a deep depression and I became a Christian as a result". That was four years ago and the most important task she faces before she dies is "share the Gospel with my dad".

An older gentleman wrote in that "I just thank God for another day. That is the only motto I need". His definition of success is certainly in line with his motto: "God will provide". A woman praised God for having a "loving husband for 63 years" and said her most important task to accomplish was to "save lots of people for Jesus". Success means "not being selfish" and her overall guiding principle is to "help others".

Caffie from Northern Atlanta, Georgia believes that "with GOD all things are possible", as she studies for her teacher certification. But a self-described conservative who is driven by the Golden Rule said that the birth of her children and "my renewed faith in God" were the two life-changing moments in her life.

One fellow wrote of his time in jail as one of two most important events in his life and "freedom" as his definition of success – as he restated that the "God Squad" best described his tribe.

Everyone else who wrote in response to our final survey identified their mottoes as "my faith in God", "Jesus died for me", "have faith and trust in GOD", "What would Jesus do?", "pray without ceasing", and "for God so loved the world that He gave His only begotten son that whosoever believes un Him should not perish but have everlasting life".

Other life-changing or defining moments included: "Accepting Christ as my Savior"; "Accepting Christ into my life by faith"; "My salvation"; "Becoming a Christian"; "The day I died and was brought back to life"; "Having faith and trusting in God"; "Being born again"; Receiving Christ"; "My baptism".: "See all of my family saved"; "Pray with all of my family into faith in Christ"; "Lead people to Christ"; "Spread the gospel"; "Lead as many people to know Jesus as I can"; "See as many temples as possible and serve within them".

Needless to say we heard and saw the same sort of thing in the most important factors in choosing friends and in the definitions of success. Here is just a smattering: "That my friends will be Christian soon"; "Help others because God has been so good to me"; "People that also love Christ and want to please Christ"; "Doing God's will"; "If they follow Christ"; "Being born-again"; "Fellow Children of God"; "Pleasing first God".

2. GO WITH THE FLOW – 23.5% OF ADULTS.

The Z-File On the Go With the Flow – *The Go With the Flow are average in every way. They possess no outstanding characteristic and they have no passion for adventure, exotic fantasies, or grand experiences. They will never skip you in line, park in a handicapped zone, boast about themselves or their kids, or scream at the umpire at a Little League game. Around half care about the environmental impact of their purchases, about the toll on workers being used to make the products they buy, and about whether or not it was made in America – but just as many do not. They are the appreciative, polite audience – not the performers. Not heavily reliant on any religion or ideological leaning, their strength comes from inside, not external forces. They author no great schemes or plans, they live each day and breathe (deeply). They are moderate and modulated. Only 44% feel that a place of worship is important to them and they are buried in the middle of tribes who prioritize eating healthy and regular exercise.*

The phrase they say which best described the meaning of their life was not surprisingly "open-minded and balanced" (30%). This is not only consistent with their total portrait but the figure is quite higher than among members of any other tribe. In a close second place came "relaxed" (28%). This is a group that has found comfort in their lives, if not confidence. They manifest very little angst in their lives and that is arguably a good thing.

Again, not surprising at all, even when it comes to political ideology, the Go With the Flow also seek balance. Two in five (41%) say they are moderates. About three in ten (29%) call themselves liberal – including 13% who are liberal on all issues, 2% just on government spending, and 14% just on social issues – while another three in ten (28%) say they are conservative, including 15% on all issues, 6% on spending, and 6% on social issues. It appears that the GWF say what they mean and mean what they say. And they say it gently.

GO WITH THE FLOW

23.5% OF ADULTS

LIFE MISSION/ MEANING

Strive for balance, moderation, zen.

FACTORS IN CHOOSING FELLOW TRIBE MEMBERS

People with balance and moderation.

DEFINITION OF SUCCESS

Achieving the middle of the road, little passion.

ONE THING MISSING TO COMPLETE LIFE

To live within means and stay in the middle of the pack.

STRENGTHENING TRIBAL BONDS

Local sporting events.

⊕ DEMOGRAPHICS

Gender For a group devoted to balance, what else could we expect but a near perfect 51-49 split between men and women?

Income The Go With the Flow are right behind the God Squad with the second highest percentage of households earning less than $50,000 (55%). Thirty-five percent earn $50,000-$100,000 and 20% are in the $100,000 plus category. (Notice how the numbers round out perfectly!)

Residence No especially notable patterns emerge with this tribe – 33% are found in larger cities, 20% in smaller cities, 33% in the sub-urbs, and 14% are rural. All about average. Three in five (62%) own their own homes.

Religion One in four (24%) of the Go With the Flow either belong to a non-affililated religious group or nothing at all, placing them among the highest in this category. Forty-five percent are Protestant, 28% are Catholic, and 3% are Jewish. Only 40% of the Protestants con-sider themselves to be Born Again (third lowest) and just 29% attend services weekly or more. Over half (54%) say they never attend any religious service.

Family About a third (32%) have children living at home (on the low side) . Nearly half (48%) are married, 28% single and never married, and 16% divorced/separated/widowed (all on the low end).

Race/Ethnicity The Go With the Flow's racial/ethnic makeup is proportional to the U.S. adult population as a whole with 66% who are white, 15% who are Hispanic, and 13% who are African American. This is just another aspect that makes this tribe average.

Age 63% are under the age of 50 (24% 18-29, 39% 30-49), but 24% are 50-64 and 13% over 65.

Employment 48% are working full or part time, only 13% are retired. Ten percent describe themselves as unemployed, 19% fear losing a job in the next year, and 23% are working at a job that pays less than a previous job.

Lifestyle Just like the God Squad, 39% are social networkers and 61% are not. Almost half (46%) have active passports, 34% say they are members of the Creative Class, and just 23% are NASCAR fans. Only 30%, among the lowest of any tribe, are weekly Wal-Mart Shoppers.

 POLITICS

The Go With the Flow tilt heavily Democrat (47%) over just 22% who are Republican. Thirty-one percent are independent or non-affiliated. Thirty-three percent are liberal –second highest of any tribe – and 29% are conservative, but they have among the highest concentrations of moderates 38%. Only 20% support the Tea Party 25% sympathize with Occupy Wall Street.

This is the only tribe where an actual majority (52%) favored the

Obamas' America over the Pauls' (20%).

On the matter of government philosophy, The Go With the Flow are evenly split with 39% understanding that, despite necessary cuts to be made, government still plays a vital role in their lives, yet 40% who believe that Americans are on the road to serfdom.

A majority (51%) are pro-choice with 42% pro-choice in all instances and 9% saying they oppose government funding for abortions. Only 24% are pro-life.

They are predictably somewhere in the middle of the pack when it comes to the importance of following politics or caring much about local government.

While they are about the same size as the God Squad, they were mainstays of the Obama re-election effort in 2012 supporting him 75% to 23%.

 ## HABITS AND ATTITUDES

Target is their favorite big box store with 26% selecting the American icon as the store they would prefer if they could only choose one. This support is followed by the runners up – J.C. Penney (15%) and Macy's (11%). Again (and again, as we will see) the stores they say would never represent who they really are were both Neiman-Marcus (27%) and Bloomingdales (19%). It is easier to find balance when the bank account is balanced. No?

This tribe's members sort of go with the flow when it comes to paying attention to food labeling and environmental impacts of food production and impacts. They are actually closer to the bottom levels of concern on issues like closely reading nutritional data (67%), looking at GMO content (36%), favoring locally grown food (52%), and regarding environmental safety standards of production (50%). But their concern is hardly absent.

This is a secular group mainly found in the middle of the pack on the major tribal attributes. Principally, they seek out "balance, zen, moderation" in themselves and others – more so than members of any other tribe. Perhaps because they are on such an even keel, they are the least likely of any tribe to feel that the American Dream is dead (only 12%). They rank very low as "edgy or rebellious", "seeking material possessions", or "needing to be the first in the neighborhood to try something new". They do rank fairly high fantasizing that they are living in a Mediterranean villa (27% do so), but, then, some places are better suited for balance than others.

GO WITH THE FLOW IN THEIR OWN WORDS

Tribal members are pretty clear about who they are and what makes them tick. This group of people who essentially seek balance are also pretty modest in what they expect from life. A West Virginian told me that his motto was "let God be your guide" and that "becoming a Christian" was one of the two most important events in his life. Success in life for him meant merely "having a good family and friends" and his only goal in life was "to retire".

A Muslim man from the Detroit area said that his personal definition of success was simply that "you get what you deserve and only what you can" and the only goal in his life was to "ensure my family's living needs".

One respondent replied that her personal motto was to be "laid back" and her most important task she would like to complete before death is "paying off all bills", while a woman from Riverside, California said her only motto was "my kids" and her most pressing task before leaving earth is "make sure my kids are well taken care of."

While one GWF said that is only motto was "don't worry about it", he did say that "fun" was important and he hoped to "become truly happy" before passing. Another defined success as merely "having what you need, that is all". Or just "work every day" and "be healthy".

Emails from GWF seemed very interested in "live and let live" and "respect of others". Michelle Irene from the State of Washington said she is driven only by the motto to "always stay calm". What are her most important criteria in choosing friends? "One close friend is fine with me", she said. But to her fellow tribe member from Southern Florida, "you are what you eat", stating that she is a vegetarian. (However she did report to us that one of her life-changing moments came when she got her "breast implants". (Another way to achieve balance, I suppose!)

But to Jill in Minnesota: "God is in control" and her most important task in life is "to make sure my kids accept Christ". How does she define success? "That Christ is glorified". Mark in northern Cook County, Illinois, said all he needs to motivate him is to "always look on the posi-

tive side, everything will end up working out". And what he needs to find friends is very simple: "must be fun to be around and nice to laugh with". He was also clear that success is only "being able to afford the things you need".

To Steve in Nashville, Tennessee, success is just "living life" and "having enough to eat and put a roof over your head. The rest is just icing on the cake". What that means to him is his motto – ""live for today, don't sweat the small stuff, and life is what you make of it".

Jennifer in Hawaii stated her personal motto is "be happy, don't worry about things you can't change" and "do unto others". Consistent with that her number one task in life is that her "kids be taken care of".

3. THE HAPPY HEDONISTS – 11.0% OF ADULTS.

The Z-File On the Happy Hedonists – *Tribal members emphasize a life that is mainly fun and meant to be enjoyed. The Happy Hedonists do it all. They dream big, they fantasize, they spend, and they want it all. They want to live life to the fullest. They are inner-directed: they dance to the beat of their own drum and they have the means to at least try to do it all. They have discretionary income so they can afford to have fun, be worldly and be mobile. They are leaders of the pack when it comes to emphasizing regular exercise (72%) and way up in the highest levels of those who eat good food. A majority think their local government is important (54%) and they – together with the Outsiders and Adventurists – love celebrity gossip (28%).*

Describing themselves as mainly "relaxed" – 32%, more than any other tribe – their sense of being relaxed comes more from a sense of living a fulfilling life. Again like the Go With the Flow they say they are "open minded and balanced". But there are unique characteristics that emerge in their word associations. For example, the 14% who say their lives are essentially "a rollercoaster" is second highest only to the Outsiders. And the 14% who told us that they are "creative and enriched" are second only to the Creators and the Adventurists.

The Happy Hedonists are by far the most liberal of the tribes – 40%. They beat out the Outsider by six percentage points and the Go With the Flow by seven, their closest rivals. And while we may wonder what the differences could be between the HH and The Adventurists, this is yet another example of their distinctions – only 30% of the latter identify as liberal. The Happy Hedonist liberals include 17% who say they are liberal all the time (also the highest), 14% who are just liberal on government spending, and 8% who are liberal mainly on social issues.

The brilliant political guru, Dick Morris, once wrote in his book <u>Inside the Oval Office</u> about his former client (then major nemesis) Bill Clinton that there was a "Saturday Night Bill" and a "Sunday Morning Bill". The former could party it up on weekends but still be so devout and close to his Maker at church services perhaps only an hour or two later. Mr. Clinton was a Happy Hedonist President.

HAPPY HEDONISTS

11% OF ADULTS

LIFE MISSION/ MEANING

Seek and have fun, live adventurously.

FACTORS IN CHOOSING FELLOW TRIBE MEMBERS

People who want as much fun as they can get.

DEFINITION OF SUCCESS

Living one's dream, life in the fast lane, as much carefree fun as possible.

ONE THING MISSING TO COMPLETE LIFE

Becoming a movie star.

STRENGTHENING TRIBAL BONDS

Group vacations, local sports events, music festivals, participating in an online chat or sharing a picture on Facebook.

DEMOGRAPHICS

Gender Almost evenly balanced, women slightly outnumber men 51% to 49%.

Income They have the second lowest percentage of low income earners (44%) and the highest concentration of those earning over $100,000 (30%). About one in four (25%) are in the middle bracket ($50,000-$100,000).

Residence **More of the Happy Hedonists live in large cities (36%) and fewer live in rural areas (11%) than any other tribe.** One in three (33%) live in suburbs and 20% live in smaller cities. Sixty-one percent own their homes.

Religion One in four (24%) are not affiliated with an organized religious group, while 33% are Catholic (the highest of all tribes) and 41% are Protestant. What is fascinating is that among the Protestants, the Happy Hedonists have the fourth highest concentration of Born Again/ Evangelicals (48%). While forty percent rarely or never attend a place of worship, 36% do attend at least weekly. And 55% say that a place of worship is very important to them -- third place among the tribes following the more predictable God Squad and Land of the Free.

Family Happy Hedonists are not entirely young but their heavier percentage of 18-29 year olds means that 32% are single/never married (third highest), but 53% are married and 41% (the highest of any tribe) have children under 17 living at home.

Race/Ethnicity They have the lowest percentage of whites of any tribe (just 58%) – 21% are Hispanic, 15% are African American, and 5% Asian.

Age Seventy-four percent are under 50 (28% 18-29 and 46% 30-49), but 26% are over 50 (19% 50-64, 7% 65+).

Employment The Happy Hedonists are the most employed tribe – 68%. Ten percent are unemployed and only 12% are retired – but 21% fear losing a job in the next 12 months (the highest among tribes) and 18% are working at a job that pays less. Forty-four percent – the highest of any tribe – call their present employment "just a gig".

Lifestyle They have the highest concentration of NASCAR fans (31%), the second highest percentage with active passports (61%), and the highest percentage who consider themselves to be social networkers (46%). Thirty-eight percent consider themselves to be in the Creative Class and 33% are in the Investor Class – both toward the high end when compared with the other tribes. They are tied with having the highest percentage of social networkers (48%). And 58% -- more than any tribe – have a passport.

 ## POLITICS

The Happy Hedonists are Democrats (49%), higher than any tribe. Only 23% are Republican (the second lowest among the tribes), and 28% are independent. With 40% claiming to be liberals, they are second highest, and their 27% conservative are the lowest. One in three are moderates (33%). They are the tribe most likely to support Occupy Wall Street

(27%) and only 22% are in support of the Tea Party.

Happy Hedonists gladly choose the Obamas' version of America 48% to 17%, yet a majority still feels America is on the road to serfdom (53%) rather than cite the good that government does (31%). The 60% who identify themselves as pro-choice on abortion is the largest majority of any tribe, however there are 26% who say they are pro-life.

Even more enthusiastically than the Go With the Flow, the Happy Hedonists voted for President Obama's re-election by a factor of 78% to 22%.

HABITS AND ATTITUDES

Tribal membership is eclectic. Some may have a higher proportion of younger people, others older or poorer. But this is a good time to remind ourselves that this is not just another demographic study. In this specific case, it is fascinating to me how stores like Wal-Mart, Sears, and Target have undergone a transformation in the public mind in recent years. In over a decade's worth of following retail, we have seen Target go from near dominance in terms of popularity to loss of public trust due to hacking of its customer base. Target is still the top choice for most of the tribes but its numbers are down. Sears has transformed from being seen as old and out of date and Wal-Mart was once the bedrock of the very conservative small town shoppers. Not any more for each.

Happy Hedonists are weekly Wal-Mart Shoppers (34%) more than any other tribe. With Wal-Mart not included in the mix, which big box stores would they select if they could only choose one? Twenty-two percent picked Target , 17% J.C. Penney, and 13% Macy's. In the early years of the century, Wal-Marts were mainly located in small town suburban settings and up-scale (whether in reality or in their minds) young people avoided them as déclassé. Since then, the Arkansas retailer has built stores in major metropolitan areas and in college towns, just as the Great Recession has hit. Wal-Mart is principally defined by price value and less by conservative values now. Happy Hedonists have shown us their willingness to live lives of "trading down" so they can afford the occasional fulfillment of their dreams via "trading up". I think this sums up their feelings about Sears as well.

Which store speaks to the Happy Hedonists the least? As with so many other tribes, Neiman-Marcus gets the nod (19%) – but now in the back-ups we see some of the old Happy Hedonist haughtiness come in – Filene's (11%) and Sears (11%).

The Happy Hedonists do care about the social impact of their food purchases. Seven in ten (70% -toward the top of the list) follow nutritional data closely, but only 34% (the lowest) pay close attention to GMO content. They are evenly split on the environmental safety impact of food production (49% follow it closely, 49% do not) but 57% care about locally produced food.

Four of five in this tribe (79%) "seek and have fun". Happy Hedonists lead the tribes for "seeking material pleasure" (44%). They also rank second as "edgy and rebellious" (right after the Adventurists) and third for being "adventurous". Three out of four (74%) seek out tribal members who want fun. On a list of events that can strengthen bonds among tribe members, the Happy Hedonists are at or very near the top on most: attending a music festival, a group vacation, getting buzzed at a tailgating party, attending a local sports event, going to a farmer's market, and conducting an online chat or visiting Facebook.

As for the biggest achievement they seek in life, they rank number one among the tribes for wanting to be a "movie star" and the lowest for wanting "to find a cure for cancer".

What if someone handed one of our Happy Hedonists a check for $5,000? He or she would be far more likely than a counterpart in the other tribes to "spend it all on the experience of my life". He or she would also be least likely to feel guilty for spending $100 or less on themselves. Only 29% of this tribe would feel guilty for spending more than a $1,000 on themselves – by far the most of any tribe. But, "Yes" they feel real love is possible, as is true with friendship, a loving family and genuine respect from others, carefree fun and a life full of meaning.

Fifty-seven percent get real satisfaction from clothes shopping and they are the head of the pack when it comes to needing to looking attractive, looking "of a higher class", "not caring what others think", and "wearing what I want to wear". Where are our Hedonists living in their wildest fantasies? More than any other tribe, 15% are "in a Beverly Hills mansion" in their wildest dreams. Their favorite store is Wal-Mart – I suppose to be able to better afford it all – but they do like Bloomingdales more than any other tribe. Happy Hedonists have to be "first to try a new product".

They are Virgos – 17% -- far more than any other tribe. They are liberals, pretty sure of themselves and libertine.

Evenly split among men and women, almost one in three have incomes of $100,000 or more – the highest among tribes. They are the most likely to live in big cities and they do love NASCAR and God (48% are Born Again). They are the second most likely of any tribe to say they are "citizens of the planet Earth", to have a passport, and least likely to be white or have a partner that is white. Just under three in ten (28%) are 18-29, but nearly half (46%) are 30-49 years of age – clearly well within the bounds of what I call the "Nike Generation", i.e. babies that were born into an America that was clearly falling apart from assassinations, the loss of a war, the loss of control of world commodities prices like oil (and coffee and sugar), babies that were "unwanted", and Watergate. "Just Do It" and have fun, right? One in seven (14%, the second highest) are not heterosexual. They are among the most likely to be Democrat and to not be Republican, among the highest to have a college background, to be liberal and not be conservative.

HAPPY HEDONISTS IN THEIR OWN WORDS

As we know, this tribe likes life. Perhaps their poster child could be the Italian actor Roberto Benigni who declared when he won Oscar for Best Actor in 1999, "I want to make love to everyone in this room". "Out of my way, full steam ahead" is how one Happy Hedonist woman defined her life's motto. Sandy from Yakima, Washington said that the most important task she would like to compete before she dies is "finding a way to live forever", while Olga from Miami said that the only thing that defines success for her is "fun", that "life is good" and her operating motto in life is "Happy Friday". Her neighbor of sorts in Saint Petersburg perhaps took it a little too far when she told us that her personal motto is "Give me that ___ (male genital organ)". That was Lisa who defined herself as a libertarian but maybe "libertine" would best describe her true character trait.

Others were high on life if not as exuberant as Lisa. "Work hard at something you love" was the motto of a young man from Southern California. His most important task he wishes to achieve in life is "to sell a screenplay and have the movie made". The most important trait he looks for in friends is "a sense of humor".

Another young man said he defines success in this life as "being happy" and his most important task to complete is "celebrate my 100th birthday". His motto is crystal clear: "live everyday as if it were your last and someday you will be right".

On the flip side, showing a duality that we noted exists in the this tribe, a very conservative Happy Hedonist summed up her motto in one word: "God".

4. THE PERSISTENTS – 19.4% OF ADULTS.

The Z-File On the Persistents – The Persistents are mainly, to outward appearances, an unremarkable lot. They are simply too busy surviving – but that in itself is a remarkable thing. They do tend to stay married and their personal tragedies are not financial in nature. They are not deeply religious, either. Their special bond is based on those who persevere and just keep pushing forward. In our open ended surveys they were the most likely to name a tragedy as one of the main defining moments in their lives – the loss of a child, an accident, a debilitating disease, a birth defect,a physical challenge, or a divorce. They are neither terribly joyous nor optimistic. Their lives are defined by struggle and that seems to occupy them the most. They are high on charitable giving because they have walked down the same road as those who are also suffering and in need. Instead of "there for the grace of God go I", they have "been there and done that".

The phrase the Persistents told us that what best describes their lives is "determined, persistent, overcoming" (32%). That is a figure that dwarfs every other tribe. They also identified most strongly with the term "work in progress" (29%) and were second highest in declaring that "hard work" (26%) is who and what they really are.

While they voted for Obama and see their world more in terms of the Obamas than the Pauls, this is still a tribe that leans more conservative than liberal. Two in five (42%) are self-described conservatives – 14% all the time, 18% on spending, and 9% just on social issues. And there are more moderates (37%) on the tribe than liberals (21%).

In many ways they are the ones we refer to as "there but for the grace of God, go I". But they transcend their experiences simply by living. They are the children's inflatable toys filled with sand on the bottom – punch them, kick them, step on them, stomp them hard and they keep bouncing right back up. Or the kid who who has stood up to the bully. Reading through their interviews, they are so impressive not for their material achievements or stunning creations, but for their ability to endure. Over and over again, they were the ones in the early open-ended surveys who told us that their motto in life was "live one day at a time".

THE PERSISTENTS

#4

19.4% OF ADULTS

LIFE MISSION/ MEANING
To persevere over life's struggles and adversity.

FACTORS IN CHOOSING FELLOW TRIBE MEMBERS
Those who deal with struggles.

DEFINITION OF SUCCESS
Survival.

ONE THING MISSING TO COMPLETE LIFE
Becoming a selfless missionary.

STRENGTHENING TRIBAL BONDS
Group vacation and school events.

DEMOGRAPHICS

Gender This is another segment dominated by women -- 54% vs. 46% who are men.

Income They have among the lowest concentration of low income households (48% earn less than $50,000), but also among the lower percentages of those over $100,000 (21%). About a third (31%) fall into the middle income categories ($50,000-$100,000).

Residence The largest portion of the Persistents live in suburbs (36%), while 23% live in big cities, and 19% live in small cities and 21% in rural areas. Two in three own their own homes.

Religion Two in five (40%) are Protestant, while 24% are Catholic and 4% are Jewish. One in three (32% are non-affiliated. Not quite half of the Protestants (45%) describe themselves as Born Again/Evangelical. One in three (28%) attend religious services at least once a week, while 50% never attend.

Family They have the fourth highest percentage of married couples (54%), while only 24% are single (the lowest percentage), and 18% are divorced or separated. Just under one in three (30%) have children living at home.

Race/Ethnicity Seven out of ten (70%) are white, while only 13% are African American, 11% are Hispanic, and 3% are Asian.

Age Just under half are 50 and older (49%), including 28% who are 50-64 and 21% over 65. Thirty-four percent are 30-49 and 17% are under 30.

Employment The Persistents are indeed working (45%) and only

16% are retired. Nine percent are unemployed. But 23% are working at a job that pays less (second highest) and 19% fear losing their jobs.

Lifestyle Three in four (75% and on the high end among tribes) do not consider themselves to be in the Investor Class, but 36% say they are in the Creative Class. About half (49%) have active passports.

 # POLITICS

While they lean heavily Democrat over Republican – 40% to 27%, with 26% describing themselves as independent – they have a high percentage of conservatives (38%)—mainly the fiscal types, like in their own households. Two in five (40% say they are moderates and only 23% are liberals. You may find them at Tea Party gatherings (26%), while only 19% sympathize with Occupy Wall Street.

The Persistents also widely favor the Obamas' America (37%) over the Pauls' (24%), but they also take the "road to serfdom" position on government by a pretty good margin (42%) over those 35% who identify more with government as a good –but damaged – force in our lives.

Almost half (47%) are pro-choice but 42% are pro-life. Seventeen percent -- more than any other tribe – identify themselves as "pro-choice only involving cases of rape".

But the Persistents are not about politics – only35% follow it closely and 38% place any real importance on their local government.

The Persistents gave President Obama a 10 point advantage – 54% to 44% in 2012-- over former Governor Romney.

HABITS AND ATTITUDES

Talk about being knocked down and having to get up. Target is the poster child store for the Persistents. Almost one in four (22%) choose it as the one store they would prefer to shop at for the rest of their lives. This is followed by Macy's (15%) and Kohl's (14%). On the flip side, the Persistents choose to not endure either Neiman-Marcus (25% say it doesn't represent who they are) or Bloomingdales (16%).

Second only to the Outsiders, the Persistents care least about locally grown/produced food (48%), although 51% do. And they are near the bottom when it comes to following closely either use of GMOs (46%) or environmental practices/impacts (52%).

They are defined by and seek out others who strongly identify with perseverance. As we learned in the open-ended surveys, there are so many people who have suffered, endured, and ultimately triumphed over some sort of personal tragedy. They have lost children, experienced divorce and separation, been forced to deal with cancer and other horrible illnesses, lost jobs, been bullied. This is a bona fide tribe. Three in four of the Persistents (75%) say that dealing with life's struggles and adversity has been very important to who they are. Almost as many (71%) look for that in others. In both cases, they are at or near the top among tribes. They are less focused on broader issues like the environment, unfair labor, and patriotism than most other tribes. They admire the "selfless missionary" as their hero.

THE PERSISTENTS IN THEIR OWN WORDS

Michelle in Rochester, Minnesota said that what personally drives her life is "it is important not to give up, to set goals and keep moving forwards". Never giving up is her definition of success as well. Another Persistent wrote that he has "to keep on truckin'" no matter what happens to him. While one woman admitted that "I wish I didn't have to put up with crap from husband!!!!!" her motto was simply "carry on". "I love my life", said another woman, "and will never give up. I have to do what I can with what I have and where I am". Two men said that they had built successful businesses and had achieved advanced degrees, but what gave their lives meaning were "health equals wealth" and "perseverance".

While an elderly woman was thankful for the 38 years of life with her husband, his death taught her simply to "do the best I can, one day at a time". Danielle from Cleveland, Ohio said she was motivated by the motto "Never stop, just never stop". The definition of success for her was "finishing what you started". And Charlotte from Salem, Oregon, said that she lost her mom, dad, and sister at a young age, but she appreciated her own life even more, wanted to only be able to pay her bills, and looked for friends who "thrust forward".

"Don't give up, always follow your heart", one woman noted, and added she is "always learning, always trying, and follows God".

A common theme throughout the messages we received from the Persistents was hardship. One respondent said that "being evicted and forced to move" was one of his life-changing events. A woman said that her husband's "quadruple bypass operation" gone awry altered her life. Divorce was traumatic for a number of people, as was widowhood.

5. THE SELF-PERFECTIONISTS – 8.3% OF ADULTS

The Z-File On The Self-Perfectionists – Members keep working for lofty personal goals, including constant self-improvement. This is a contrarian tribe. They are non-religious, cynical, self-centered, unenthusiastic about church, family, music, group vacations, spiritual retreats, small dinner parties, tailgating or school events. Beware: don't invite them over for Canasta or a casual game of Twister. They are moderate in their politics, artsy, and focused almost entirely on themselves .They have the highest divorce/separation rate of any of the tribes. They actually prefer to be alone. For the rest of us, that is okay.

The three dominant defining characteristics for the Self-Perfectionists are "hard work" (23%), "determined, persistent, overcoming" (23%), and "open-minded and balanced" (21%) – but the two phrases where they topped all other tribes were "ambitious" (14%) and "accomplished" (14%). This is a goal-driven tribe and their theme song could very well be "ain't nothing going to break my stride, ain't nothing going to slow me down, oh no, I got to keep on moving."

About one out of three Self-Perfectionists (34%) say they are conservative all the time, with another 7% conservative just on government spending and 3% on social issues. But 26% are liberals – 10% all the time, 6% on spending and 9% on social issues. Forty percent are moderates. But you don't want to engage them in politics anyway. They know it all.

Like the Creators, they are most likely to define themselves as a "work in progress" but their drive is based less on the desire to create ideas, works, or things, than to mold and shape themselves – to be all they themselves can be. They are determined and persistent but in a goal-oriented way. Narcissists, maybe? Solipsists? Definitely. They will sing their aria through life – "I,I, I...Me,Me, Me". Sure they want to write the Great American Novel, but it is for the headlines not the reviews. They like being alone because they are their own best (and perhaps only) friend. Charitable gifts? Only if there is a headline or visible recognition.

THE **SELF-PERFECTIONISTS**

8.3% OF ADULTS

LIFE MISSION/
MEANING
To be authentic, genuine.

FACTORS IN CHOOSING
FELLOW TRIBE MEMBERS
Sticking closely to family and loved ones.

DEFINITION
OF SUCCESS
To be contrarian, above the crowd.

ONE THING MISSING
TO COMPLETE LIFE
Writing the Great American Novel.

STRENGTHENING
TRIBAL BONDS
Being alone, even with others.

DEMOGRAPHICS

Gender There are slightly more men than women (55%-45%).

Income Nearly half (47%) are in the under $50,000 income bracket, one in four (27%) earn $50,000-$100,000, and 23% are over $100,000.

Residence There are no distinct characteristics here: 28% live in large cities, 23% in small cities, 33% in suburbs, and 16% are rural. They have the second lowest concentration of homeowners (62%).

Religion The Self-Perfectionists have the second highest concentration of non-affiliated (44%) and are from there evenly balanced between Protestants (27%) and Catholics (25%). Forty-four percent of the already small group of Protestants consider themselves to be Born Again/Evangelical (34%). And only 27% attend services at least weekly (third lowest).

Family Almost half are married (47%), while 41% (by far the highest of all the tribes) are single and never married. However, one in three of have children under 17 living at home (33%).

Race/Ethnicity Sixty-four percent are white, while 14% Hispanic, 16% African American, 5% Asian.

Age Thirty-eight percent are 30-49 years of age (third highest) and another 34% are under 30. They are the second highest percentage of tribes with people under 50. Nineteen percent are 50-64 and only 9% are over 65.

Employment Because so many of the Self-Perfectionists are under 50, only 15% are retired. But 57% are working full or part time. Only 15% fear losing a job and only 17% are working at a job that pays less.

Lifestyle They are most certainly not NASCAR fans (only 17%, the lowest). They are not greatly represented within either the Investor Class (26%) or the Creative Class (34%). Almost a majority (54%) have active passports – the third highest. One in four (27%) do shop weekly at Wal-Mart.

 POLITICS

This is another Democratic-leaning tribe – 37% to 26% Republicans – but 36% are independents. Forty-three percent are moderates, the highest of any group. Twenty-six percent are liberal and 31% are conservative. They are very near the bottom in their lack of support for either the Tea Party (18%) or Occupy Wall Street (20%).

Only one in three (34%) say they prefer the America of the Obamas and a lot fewer -- 23% -- select that of the Pauls. This Democratic but slightly conservative-leaning tribe shows its colors on the question of government with 61% saying we Americans are on the road to serfdom while 28% feel government is basically more good than bad.

Almost half (46%) are pro-choice while 42% are pro-life.

The Self-Perfectionists supported Mr. Obama 57% to 40% over Mr. Romney.

 HABITS AND ATTITUDES

The Self-Perfectionists may seek the ultimate in personal improvement and self-actualization, but they don't seem to want to pay Neiman-Marcus prices for it. One in four of the Self-Perfectionists (25%) are just not buying it (literally as well as figuratively).

Members of this tribe care more deeply than any other tribe, with the exception of the Creators and the Adventurists, about the food they eat. Three in four (76%) watch closely the nutritional data about food before purchasing and 55% pay close attention to the environmental practices involved in the food they eat. They are also at or near the top of the tribes who care about locally produced food (57%). That caution does not, however, extend to the use of GMOs (only 43%).

This is not a very pleasant tribe to be around. They have the lowest or near lowest ratings on every one of the attributes listed in the survey. While 56% do rate "authenticity/honesty" as most or very important, that is still the lowest of any tribe. They don't even enjoy a trip to the farmers' market, for God's sake. More than every other tribe, except for the Happy Hedonists, they would spend a $5,000 windfall on themselves. Only one in four (26%) say they have already achieved true love – by far the lowest.

A whopping 58% -- more than any other tribe – say they "are living (their) own dream".More than any other tribe, however, they dream about that Mediterranean villa and they are the very top in fantasizing about living in a New York City penthouse. One in three want others to think they are the smartest person they know – which is high. One in six hope to write the great American novel – the most of any tribe.

They wouldn't be caught dead in Wal-Mart – only 27% prefer the Arkansas icon, among the lowest.

THE SELF-PERFECTIONISTS IN THEIR OWN WORDS

Leave it to a Self-Perfectionist to cite his motto quoting 17th century author Blaisé Pascal in French: "Le couer a ses raisons que la reason ne connait point" ("the heart has its reasons that reason knows nothing of"). This is the same person who responded that he had no other important tasks he would like to complete before he dies because he had "already accomplished them all". Debra in New York City said that her motto was simply "love, health, and money" and one of her two most important events in life was "hitting one million dollars". (The other, by the way, was marriage). "Wealth and health defined success for her and she chose only friends who had "positive attitudes".

A man who said that he retired at 50 said that his motto was "to be the best" and "to be the best you can be" defined success for him. And a woman answered both these questions with the simple one word response: "results". Johanna in Orlando, Florida said she was driven by and explained her life by "living life to the fullest". The only task remaining for her to complete was to "travel the world". Alyssa in Altoona, Pennsylvania said that "she keeps on pushing" and one of the events that changed her life was "buying my first car".

We saw references to wealth from both those who said they were liberals and conservatives – and some followed with the definition of success to be able to make money.

6. THE ADVENTURISTS – 12.2% OF ADULTS.

The Z-File On the Adventurists – *Do not confuse the Adventurists with Happy Hedonists. Members are curious, always exploring the new, and share a passion for the experimental; they are restless. Life is one big joy ride for them. They want it all and they want it now. They are not as selfish as the Happy Hedonists or the One True Path—but they have less time for God than either tribe. The Adventurists have families, have dealt with adversity, and seek love and friendship. They are the ones most likely of all the tribes to seek and find the pony in the trials and tribulations of life. They also shop a lot at Wal-Mart which means they too probably trade-down to afford the trading-up they love and dream about so much. They also are top investors. There is both a libertarian (and even libertine) streak in this tribe –with so many 30-49 year olds, half belong to what I have described as the Nike Generation. Next to the Outsiders, they show the least interest in the American flag (only 57%) but less out cynicism and more from a mobile and global mindset.*

One of the main things that makes the Adventurists adventurous is that they told us that is what they are. One in five (21%) said that word best described the meaning of their life. The next highest group to identify with the word was the Happy Hedonists who barely hit 10% -- then no one else reached 7%. They are also "open-minded and balanced (24%) and a "work in progress" (24%), along with bits and pieces of other characteristics . But it is the wanderlust that spells out who they are and what makes them different. They are also, to a great degree, pretty cocky, with 20% -- the highest of any tribe – saying what best describes them is they are "always interesting." And their dream home is neither homey (their "current home") nor a relaxing getaway to kick off their shoes and relax ("a Mediterranean villa"). This tribe wants "a New York City penthouse" or a "Beverly Hills mansion".

THE ADVENTURISTS
#6

12.2% OF ADULTS

LIFE MISSION/ MEANING

Across the highways and byways seeking kicks at every turn.

FACTORS IN CHOOSING FELLOW TRIBE MEMBERS

Adventuresome, optimists, fun-seekers.

DEFINITION OF SUCCESS

A Beverly Hills mansion or a New York City penthouse.

ONE THING MISSING TO COMPLETE LIFE

Becoming a movie star, a billionaire, or a great inventor; a life of meaning and freedom to pursue passions.

STRENGTHENING TRIBAL BONDS

Group vacation, dinner party, music festival, shopping for clothes.

 **DEMOGRAPHICS**

Gender Three in five (59%) are men.

Income Over one in four (28%, on the higher side) earn over $100,000; 30% earn $50,000-$100,000, while 42% earn less than $50,000.

Residence Thirty-one percent live in large cities (second highest) and only 16% are rural (second lowest). One in six live in small cities (18%) and 35% are suburban. Two in three (64%) are homeowners.

Religion Thirty-nine percent are non-affiliated, 31% identify as Protestant, 26% are Catholic, and 4% are Jewish. Forty-three percent of Protestants are Born Again and 42% never attend religious services.

Family One in three (31%) are single, while 53% are married. Thirty-seven percent have children uder 17 living at home (second highest).

Race/Ethnicity Two thirds (68%) are white, 15% are Hispanic, 9% are African American, and 4% are Asian.

Age They are the second youngest group (70% under age 50)—31% of the total 18-29 and 39% 30-49.

Employment Three in five are working (59%, the second highest) and only 11% are retired.

One in five either fear losing their job in the next 12 months (21%) or work at a job that pays less (19%). Forty-three percent – the second highest among the tribes – consider their current job to be "just a gig".

Lifestyle The Adventurists lead the tribes as members of the Investor Class (38%) and are tied for the lead as social networkers (46%). They also are the most likely to shop at least weekly at Wal-Mart (33%) and to have a passport (62%). They are number two in being fans of NASCAR (26%). They are second highest among tribes for shopping weekly at Wal-Mart and they are tied with the Happy Hedonists as the most having a passport (57%).

They rank second among all tribes for their interest in eating healthy food (76%) – topped only by the Creators.

 ## POLITICS

Again they are not Happy Hedonists. The Happy Hedonists are far more likely to identify with the America of Barack and Michelle Obama, while the Adventurists are about evenly split between that of the Obamas and the Pauls. The explanation can mainly be found in their ideological preferences. Thirty percent identify themselves as liberals (12% all the time, only 4% on spending, and 13% just on social issues) and 34% are conservatives. But the conservatives are predominantly drawn from those who just identify that way on the basis of government spending – 20%, while 10% are conservative all the time and only 4% are conservative on social issues. One in three (36%) are moderates. But libertarians and libertarian-leaning candidates need to find their Adventurists because that is a good source of supporters.

One of just two tribes to reach 50% claiming to prefer the Obamas' version of America (50%), the Adventurists still have 30% who like the

Pauls. Yes, they are Democrats – 42% feel that government does good things – but still there is that libertarian sensibility with 50% fearing the road to serfdom.And the Adventurists are indeed pro-choice (53%) while 35% say they are pro-life. Their interest in both local government and in politics mirrors that of the Happy Hedonists.

Even though the Adventurists are mainly liberal and Democrat, their support for President Obama's re-election was less present in 2012. They voted for Mitt Romney by a factor of 48% to 46%, with 6% voting for independent candidates.

HABITS AND ATTITUDES

The Adventurists have the drive, the spirit, the cash and love of the big life -- but they prefer to do their ultimate shopping experience at either Target (26%) or Macy's (15%). This is the ultimate defining characteristic of those who trade down so they can trade up. The also prefer to spend money on experiences, not stuff. But there is another side to these fun-lovers.

One half (49%) of the Adventurists pay close heed to the use of GMOs in the food they buy and 59% care deeply about nutritional data. More than any other tribe, they closely follow the environmental impact of the production process (65%) – more than any other tribe.

Aside from God and Faith and duty (which rate the lowest among the tribes), they seem to want as much out of life as they can get. Four in five (78%) want adventure and the same (79%) want that from fellow tribe members. They are also the most optimistic (77%), the most rebellious (35%), and are the second highest preferring fun and enjoyment and attaining possessions.

The Adventurists are at or near the very top in being satisfied by a wide array of experiences – music festivals, group vacations, dinner parties, tailgating, and online chats. Forty percent (the second highest among the tribes) call themselves "individualists" and they are the most likely to want to dive to the bottom of the ocean to explore or become a movie star (second highest).

They are also at or very near the top when it comes to enjoying life: achieving real love, pursuing carefree fun, personal fulfillment, living a life full of meaning, and even shopping for clothes. At the same time, they care the most about environment and human rights of labor when shopping and they are number one among tribes in the need to look attractive, look a higher class than they are, not care what anyone thinks, and look "all business". Give them $5,000 and over half would spend it on their family – a high rating.

THE ADVENTURISTS IN THEIR OWN WORDS

Let's kick this off with the woman who said that "my sexual awakening" was one of the two most important events in her life. The self-described political progressive told us that her guiding motto was "cautiously adventurous" and that her definition of success was always being "calm, cool and collected". For Sam in Southern, California, the motto that drives him is "I want it now" and his most important unfinished task in life is merely to "date the hottest babe in America". Not surprisingly both the most important factors in choosing friends and his definition of success that guides him is "sexy and rich". Any other aspects of his life worth sharing? Sam replied "it is too hot to handle".

One woman wrote that she is driven by the motto to "create your own destiny" and that doing a "road trip" was the most important task she needs to fulfill in her life. There was the more subdued fellow who said that "marriage and being a father" were the two most important events in his life, his life-changing moments, but he just had "to travel to Europe" before he died. In fact he told us that he just "loves to travel" as much as he can. For him success is "always learning".

This was underscored by John in Westchester County, New York who described his motto as "learning something new every day". John loves to hike but his life's ambition is "to publish a book". Nick in neighboring Connecticut said that before he dies he "will move to Guatemala to open a business and help the hungry and poor". His motto is "live each day like it's your last – one day you will be right" and, while "sticking by my partner – in good times and bad – is one of the two most important life-changing moments for him, the other is "contemplating moving abroad". Success for Nick? "People who follow a path of their own, entrepreneurship and innovation, and the most successful of those are respected and loved for who they are and not what they do".

7. LAND OF THE FREE – 33.2% OF ADULTS.

The Z-File On the Land of the Free – *Basically, this is an average group, conservative, traditional, secular, hardworking, male, rural and small town. Half (49%) have not attended at least some college. Listen closely and you can hear them humming Archie and Edith Bunker's anthem, "Those Were the Days". You know: "when girls were girls and men were men. Mister, we could use a man like Herbert Hoover again."They are the Cold Warriors, John McCain's brigades. Get to your nearest Applebee's at 4PM and you are likely to run into them there. But one respondent summed up the entire tribe perfectly: "Our freedom as Americans is what defines us; we are always prepared, rational, independent." They are ready to put up their dukes for truth, justice and the American way. With 30% who are either veterans or live with a veteran of the armed forces, they rank number one in this category.*

Basic traditional values characterize the Land of the Free. And that is precisely what they told us. What are their top identifiable characteristics that define who they are. One in three (31%) said "honorable and trustworthy", followed by "freedom" (24%), and "hard work (21%).

Unlike the failed effort by General Motors to revive the Oldsmobile, members of the Land of the Free are "your grandfather's" conservatives. Like the God Squad, a majority (55%) are self-described conservatives, with the lion's share (35%) saying they are conservative all the time, another 11% just on spending issues, and 5% only on social issues. Only 14% are self-described liberals – 6% all the time, 3% on spending, and 5% on social issues. And 26% are moderates.

#7

LAND OF THE FREE

33.2% OF ADULTS

LIFE MISSION/ MEANING

Duty and responsibility, simplicity, and no frills.

FACTORS IN CHOOSING FELLOW TRIBE MEMBERS

Those who live authentically and have a sense of duty and responsibility.

DEFINITION OF SUCCESS

Live free or die, patriotism.

ONE THING MISSING TO COMPLETE LIFE

Find a cure for cancer.

STRENGTHENING TRIBAL BONDS

Attending a place of worship, a group vacation, a school event.

DEMOGRAPHICS

Gender More men than women (52%-48%).

Income About half are found in the lowest income bracket (48%), one third (32%) in the $50,000-$100,000 bracket, and only 21% over $100,000.

Residence Less than one in five (19%) can be found in large cities (the second lowest), while more (21%) live in small cities, 38% in suburbs, and 22% in rural areas (tied for highest). Seventy-three percent own their own home, the highest.

Religion With 45% Protestant they are in third place among tribes. There are about as many nonaffiliated (26%) as there are Catholics (25%). Four percent are Jews. Exactly half of the Protestants consider themselves to be Born Again. Over one third are at least weekly attendees of religious services (36%). Three in five (60%) say a place of worship is very important to them – 23 points lower but still in second place to the God Squad.

Family Sixty percent are married (the highest) and only 18% are single never married (the lowest). One in five (19%) are divorced or separated.

Race/Ethnicity **They have the highest percentage of whites of any tribe (84%), but 6% are Hispanic, 5% African American, and 3% Asian.**

Age With 57% over the age of 50, they are the oldest of the tribes. The 30% who are over 65 are number one. But there are 12% who are 18-29 and 31% who are 30-49.

Employment More retirees are found among the Land of the Free than in any of the other tribes (19%), but 41% are still working. One in five (20% each) are either afraid of losing their job in the next 12 months or working at a job that pays less than a previous job.

Lifestyle They are present in a number of activities as 23% are fans of NASCAR, 29% are social networkers, 26% are Investor Class, 34% are Creative Class, and 41% have active passports. One in four are frequent Wal-Mart Shoppers (27%).

 ## POLITICS

This is a Republican bastion – 37% identify themselves as Republican and only 30% Democrats. Twenty-seven percent call themselves independent. They have the second highest concentration of conservatives (55%) and the lowest percentage of liberals (14%), with one in three saying they are moderates (32%).

By 2 to 1, the Land of the Free favors Ron and Rand Paul's America (41%) over the Obamas' (19%). Two out of three (66%, among the highest) worry about government leading Americans down the road to serfdom, while only 21% admit that government does good things and employs many people. Over half (51%) are pro-life, with 39% saying they are pro-choice.

But the defining characteristic of the Land of the free is their regard for the American flag – 86% say it is very important to them, by far the most among the tribes.

Bedrock conservatives, the Land of the Free gave Mitt Romney a 17 point advantage over Barack Obama, 57% to 40%. They are tied with the God Squad – 32% each – as the top supporters of the tea Party, but at 10% they are the lowest among supporters of Occupy Wall Street.

 ## HABITS AND ATTITUDES

The Land of the Free also prefer Target but their 20% is the lowest of any tribe. Kohl's (15%) and Macy's (11%) are next but the 9% who embrace Sear's as the one store they would pick if they only had one choice is the highest of any tribe. One in three of the Land of the Free (32%) eschew any identification with Neiman-Marcus, as do 20% reject Bloomingdales.

While over half (54%) may turn their heads away from the environmental impact of the food they eat and only 39% pay any attention to the use of GMOs, 65% pay close attention to nutritional data and 60% prefer to buy locally grown food.

The last time this tribe was edgy or rebellious was probably 1776. Their chief attributes are duty and honor (78%), no frills simplicity (75%), and faith in God (66%). They seek out the same in fellow tribal members – including a great emphasis on authenticity, as well.

This group of patriots feels that the American Dream is barely breathing (58%, more than any other tribe), but they still wholeheartedly believe in it. They do indeed care about the environment and labor in their consumer products, just not as much as most other tribes. For them, "Made in America" is the most important value they look for when shopping.

They are very heterosexual and white.

LAND OF THE FREE IN THEIR OWN WORDS

Andrea from Lynchburg, Virginia stated that her personal motto was "the freedom to keep going", that she wanted to be free to travel around the world and she defined success by "never stop learning new things". But she also described herself as very conservative and that she "loves life but I distrust people". So she felt more comfortable in this tribe, not the Adventurists. But then there was the older gentleman who believed with all his heart that he should "live and let live" and defined success by "being yourself" and he actually, unlike Andrea, wanted "to empower as many people as possible" before he died – so un-Andrea.

We heard and read a wide variety of things – mainly simplicity, home-spun, family-oriented values. But this tribe cherished liberty above all else. To one feisty older gentleman, "success is the achievement of as much independence as possible. Not just financial, but independence to do whatever you want without having to answer to anyone". This was perfectly consistent with both his motto – "dismiss the supernatural and embrace the rational" and his life-changing "decision to be a self-employed engineer". When choosing his friends he said he tried to "avoid people devoted to dogma of any kind". The Founding Fathers would be so proud of him.

Jeffrey from the suburbs of Trenton, New Jersey, only wanted to talk about his family and work – hut cherished the freedom to live in a country where he was free from worry. Robert from DuPage County, Illinois, said he was guided by "freedom", the need to live a full life, and was "very conservative" because he hated anything that impeded his opportunity to accomplish that.

Ryan is a libertarian from Eureka, California who is guided by the motto "keep on keeping on". He dreams of buying a house and "getting my dream job". Wendy from outside Rochester, New York said she is a progressive/very liberal but cherished her life in this country. "If something is worth living for, then it is worth dying for". Rich from somewhere in lovely Maine has a very simple LOF motto: "I did it my way". A firm believer in the American Dream, he feels he is living it. "I was lucky to get into data processing early in my career and met my beautiful wife". For him, "work hard and be rewarded and being honest" pretty much sums up his life.

A self-described conservative Robin from Sioux City, Iowa said her motto is "do what you gotta do". One of her life-changing moments was "the day I gave my life to Christ".

David from Kansas City, Missouri felt that "one of the primary molders of my character has been my service in the military". A conservative, he said he was driven by the motto "treat others with dignity and respect and expect the same from others". Another conservative, Lori from Cleveland, Ohio, saw being a Land of the Free as meaning the ability to focus on helping others and being a good person as the freedom to not have to worry about the things those less fortunate must focus on.

One man who emailed us said his motto is "we can be free to go anywhere, do anything, and everything freely". And Steve from Los Angeles, California "success is the ability to define your own success".

8. THE ONE TRUE PATH – 13.4% OF ADULTS.

The Z-File On the One True Path – They are very focused and reject anything they don't see as clearly authentic, real, creative, honest. They are the new face of evangelicals in the United States. They are conservative but they care about the environment and human rights. They are younger and hipper. They are also more broad-minded than the God Squad and the Dutifuls. This tribe is inner-directed and self-assured. One in three are either Hispanic (18%, second highest) or African American (14%, second highest).

They follow a strict code. How best to define their life's meaning? More than any other tribe (34%) they called themselves "honest and trustworthy". At the same time, second only to the Dutifuls, they said "compassionate, generous, accommodating to others" (25%) best told their story. They are also "purposeful and meaningful" (22%) and "determined, persistent, overcoming" (23%). But what truly makes them unique is that they strongly identify as both "blessed and saved" (24%) as well as "open-minded and balanced" (21%). In short, they are Millennial Millennialists, to some degree. They are not your – to dredge the well-worn Oldsmobile advertising slogan -- grandfather's evangelicals.

Like the Land of the Free and the God Squad, they are more conservative, but just not to the degree as the other tribes – 48% total, with 29% all the time, 4% on spending, and 14% just on social issues.

They are the new face of Born Again/Evangelical conservatives. They are indeed conservative in their lives and in their hearts. They drink the Kool-Aid when it comes to God, Guns, and Gonads, but they just don't want to talk about these things anymore. They tell their pastors – and their humble pollsters – that they are more concerned about poverty in their communities, global warming ("man's stewardship of God's Earth"), and making a difference in their world. They are even more concerned about child labor and the human rights in fellow Christians in developing countries. They are younger, family-oriented, and desirous of living a meaningful life. The One True Path are not dogmatic – just simpler, more open-minded. They are the difference between those who flocked to James Dobson, Pat Robertson and Jerry Falwell yesterday and those who identify with Rick Warren and Joel Osteen today.

#8
ONE **TRUE PATH**

13.4% OF ADULTS

LIFE MISSION/ MEANING
Authenticity, duty and family.

FACTORS IN CHOOSING FELLOW TRIBE MEMBERS
Authenticity, perseverance against life's struggles, faith in God.

DEFINITION OF SUCCESS
To be the smartest person in the room.

ONE THING MISSING TO COMPLETE LIFE
Become a president or CEO.

STRENGTHENING TRIBAL BONDS
Place of worship, music festival.

DEMOGRAPHICS

Gender Women outnumber men among the One True Path 53% to 47%.

Income Over half (52%) earn under $50,000, while 29% are in the middle income bracket, and 19% make $100,000 or more.

Residence Twenty-seven percent live in large cities, 18% in small cities, 36% in suburbs, and 20% rural. Two thirds (65%) own their home.

Religion The OTP have the third highest concentration of Protestants (60%) and the second lowest percentage of Jews (2%). Under one in four are Catholic (22%) and 16% are nonaffiliated. **Three in five are Born Again and 36% attend religious services at least weekly – both second highest.** They are fourth on putting great faith in a place of worship (54%, just behind, most interestingly, the Happy Hedonists).

Race/Ethnicity Only 71% are white, while 14% are African American, 12% Hispanic, and 3% Asian.

Family A majority are married (52%), while 22% are single and never married, and 19% are divorced or separated. Only one in four (5%) have children under 17 living at home.

Age Thirty-one percent are between the ages of 30-49 and 20% are under 30. One in four (25%) are 50-64 and 24% are over 65.

Employment Only 14% of this tribe are retired but 39% are working full or part time.

Lifestyle **Thirty-four percent are social networkers – low for a younger tribe – and only 21% are in the Investor Class, 41%**

have a passport, 27% are in the Creative Class, and 26% shop at least weekly at a Wal-Mart. There is nothing remarkable about any of these except that they are average in their distributions. They rank fourth for not attending college (48%).

 ## POLITICS

While almost evenly matched between Democrats (33%) and Republicans (30%) – with 25% independent – they rank third among tribes identifying themselves as conservative (43%) while only 19% consider themselves to be liberal. Two in five (38%) are moderates.

Only one in four (26%) give thumbs up to the Obamas' America, while 36% favor the Pauls. Sixty-eight percent (the second highest of any of the tribes, say that government spending is leading Americans down the road to serfdom while only 19% feel government is a good thing.

About half (51%) are pro-life second highest -- and 35% are pro-choice.

The One True Path lead in their emphasis on the importance of following politics (44%). One is four are sympathetic to the Tea Party and just 13% -- tied for lowest with the God Squad – sympathize with Occupy Wall Street.

The One True Path voted for Obama 50% to 46% in 2012, but it could be that they feared some of the excesses of the Republican candidates as expressed during the twenty nationally televised debates.

🛒 HABITS AND ATTITUDES

And it's Target for the One True Path with 28%, followed by Costco (15%). Twenty-six percent feel Bloomingdales is least like them, distantly followed by Neiman Marcus at 16%. Their "one true path" appears to be heading toward saving money as well as saving souls.

Concerns about food quality food and healthy production standards know no ideology or age limitations. The evangelical OTP care very much about nutritional data (71%), GMOs (51%), locally produced food (64%), and the environmental impact of food production (58%). What sets this group apart is their quest for authenticity. Ninety-percent (tied for highest) cite this as the most important attribute. At the same time, they place the highest of any tribe's value on family (91%). This is in sharp contrast with the only 29% high importance on fun. Nine in ten (90%) also seek out authenticity in other members of their tribe – both the highest value and the highest of any tribe. They also place a high premium on their fellow tribesmen's simplicity (68%, number one) and perseverance (75%, number one).

The OTP's tribal bonds can be strengthened best at a place of worship (71%), but they also can be enhanced at a music festival (44%, tied for highest with Happy Hedonists), getting buzzed at a tailgating party (25%, the third highest after the Happy Hedonists and the Adventurists), attending a local sports event, a school event for their children, or on Facebook – all high.

They have such a positive view of themselves and the American Dream that 11% aspire to become either President of the United States or the

CEO of a company – the most of any tribe. This group even finds their job fulfilling – 56%, second highest of any tribe. They also fantasize about living in a Beverly Hills mansion (second highest) and being the smartest person others know. They aspire to being the first in their neighborhood to try something new (third highest and they barely have any Mac users (.3%, the lowest of any tribe).

THE ONE TRUE PATH IN THEIR OWN WORDS

This is an eclectic group, to a great degree God-centered but also modern, secular, and ambitious. Thus, for Teresa Ann in Birmingham, Alabama, her most important task before she leaves this earth is "be rich" and she defines "money" as the definition of success that guides her life. But for Chad in Bloomingdale, Illinois, who unlike Teresa's very liberal politics said he is "very conservative", his guiding light is brightened by the Golden Rule. He would like only to buy his "mom a new home" as his great unfinished task" and success for him is "hard work and the will to succeed". Michael of Phoenix, Arizona said the main thing he would like others to know about his life is that "it's been rewarding and God is in my life at all times". He wants only to "keep helping others" and wants people to be able to say of him when he dies "that I was always trying to help someone out".

Joel Osteen must be the patron saint of this tribe. One man wrote that his personal motto is he is "driven by money" and that his definition of success is "making lots of money so I get everything I want". A bit of a cynic, He said his motto is "in God we trust, all others pay cash". He also related that his too most important events in life were "my finger on the trigger and cop walks into the bar – and – my father in a mental hospital and I told him I'm leaving for California. Instantly he was cured". Even though he identified with the One True Path he said the most important factors in choosing his friends was "the scripture, trust no man". "Life is hard, then you die" is how he ended his email. Another man said simply "God be with you" was his motto.

Cindy from the San Gabriel in California noted that she is driven by the notion that "less is more" and success for her means "living in the moment" and "dumping the ego".

9. THE OUTSIDERS – 5.8% OF ADULTS.

The Z-File On The Outsiders – They share a spirit of rebelliousness, anger at the system, and never 'let the bastards grind you down'. John Donne may have written that no man is an island, but he probably never conducted polls and asked people how they really felt. Holden Caulfield is all grown up – sort of. And Lena Dunham isn't. They are iconoclastic, cynical, bored, lonely, individualistic, and bitter. They have experienced hard times, are still down and out, down on their luck, pessimistic, not terribly adventurous or entrepreneurial. They have lost jobs or work for less and they feel it because they tend to be women with kids working for lower wages. My sense is that Lucy van Pelt of Peanuts is all grown up and an Outsider. A sign appears on their door: "Don't Bother Me. Am Out to Lunch". They may dream of creating or writing, but that train has probably already left the station for them.

They don't strengthen their tribal bonds from anything at all. They don't believe in the American Dream and do not think it is alive and well. Only 5% say they are presently living their Dream. No other tribe is even close to them. They are the living embodiment of a Roger Waters song: they don't need no education, no God, no perseverance, no fun, no balance, no adventure, no simplicity, no authenticity.

If you ever lived in a dorm, these were the people who lived down the hall who played cards until they flunked out of school. They played not because it was fun. Instead, they seemed to be endlessly waiting for Godot. They had a cynical sense of humor – the stuff of which pro- duced the likes of Lenny Bruce, Richard Pryor, and George Carlin. But it wasn't going to happen for them. They are the Hoop Dreamers of

Standup Comedy. They haven't made it. Can you picture Bruce, Carlin or Pryor driving your kids' school bus? Arranging a small business loan at a community bank? Or even applying for a job? They are growing up slowly and are misfits. Generally, they don't give a shit about anything or anybody. Unless they strike gold. They also wouldn't mind that Mediterranean villa but it isn't going to happen. They may be very witty in a biting way, but they are not having fun. And they are much more concerned with self to care about others, about issues, about social networking.

The Outsiders appear to embrace their own imperfections. One in three (33%) say they are best described as a "work in progress" – significantly more than any other tribe. One in four (25%) felt that are best seen as "confusing and confounding." No other tribe reaches 6% on this one and most are in the 1%-3% range. By far and away, the 20% who say their lives are a "rollercoaster" is substantially more than any other tribe, as are the 15% who say their lives are best summed up as being "unpredictable".

On the other hand, a few (but only a very few) say they are "compassionate, generous, and accommodating to others (14%), "peaceful" (14%), and "honorable and trustworthy" (16%).

They do tend to be more liberal when it comes to self-identification – 39% to only 21% conservative and 27% moderate -- but their conservatism is mainly on spending with only 5% full-time conservative and 4% on social issues. They are not carefree libertarians. Rather they appear to be anti-institution, bitter, and lean towards the words of an early 20th Century Mexican revolutionary slogan: "down with whoever's up."

THE **OUTSIDERS**

#9

5.8% OF ADULTS

LIFE MISSION/ MEANING
To be an individualist.

FACTORS IN CHOOSING FELLOW TRIBE MEMBERS
Authenticity.

DEFINITION OF SUCCESS
A great artist or inventor.

ONE THING MISSING TO COMPLETE LIFE
To live in a castle in Europe.

STRENGTHENING TRIBAL BONDS
Being alone.

DEMOGRAPHICS

Gender Women outnumber men 56% to 44%.

Income The Outsiders have the greatest percentage of low income earners of any tribe – 58% -- and the lowest percentage of high income earners – 16%. Twenty-six percent are in the $50,000-$100,000 bracket.

Residence Thirty-seven percent – tied for second place – live in the suburbs, 21% are in big cities, and 24% in small cities. Only half own their homes – much much lower than any other tribe.

Religion About half (48%) are either identified with no religion or are nonaffiliated – by far number one in this category. Only 21% are Catholic and 27% are Protestant. They have the highest concentration of Jews (5%). Only thirty--four percent of the small number of Protestants consider themselves to be Born Again—by far the lowest -- and only 23% of all Outsiders attend weekly or more religious services, again the lowest. Three in five (61%) rarely or never attend, both number one. But half say a place of worship is important to them – perhaps as seen from the outside.

Race/Ethnicity Seventy percent are white, while 10% each are African American or Hispanic and 4% are Asian.

Family They have the lowest percentage who are married (46%), while 36% have never been married and 12% are divorced or separated. One in three (34%) have children living at home.

Age Three out of four (73%) are under 50 – 38% are 30-49 years of age and another 35% are under 30. Twenty-seven percent are over 50.

Employment While half are working (43%), 21% are unemployed by far the most of any tribe. Twenty-eight percent each are either afraid of losing their current job or working for less – both also by far the highest among the tribes.

Lifestyle **They have the lowest percentage who consider their current jobs to be a career (32%),** as well as the lowest percentages of social networkers (26%), Investor Class (17%), and have active passports (29%). But 36% do feel they are in the Creative Class. Eighty percent are not NASCAR fans and they have the second lowest percentage of social networkers, even though they are so young. Just 18% identify themselves as members of the Investor Class – by far the lowest – and only 36% have a passport, also the lowest.

 ## POLITICS

One third (34%) say they are liberal, with 35% saying they are moderates and 31% conservative. There are more Democrats (34%) than Republicans (22%) and independents (26%). Only 20% support the Tea Party (the lowest), while 20% identify with Occupy Wall Street, both among the lowest.

Their governing ideology, however, still favors the "Don't Tread On Me" philosophy of the Ron and Rand Paul (33%) over the government activist approach of Barack and Michelle Obama (25%). Plus, they are tied at 44% over identifying government as fundamentally a good thing vs. pushing Americans down the road to serfdom.

But don't tread on the Outsiders' right to choice in abortion – at least

50% of them – while 19% say they are pro-life. From what I see, they lack the "audacity of hope."

Outsiders voted for Mitt Romney – go figure, keep us guessing – 47% to 45% -- and 7% supported another candidate.

 ## HABITS AND ATTITUDES

They may not want to be in the mainstream but when it comes to making a choice for the one big box store, the Outsiders are in the same big box with mostly every other tribe. They choose Target (28%) over Macy's (16%), and Kohl's (15%). However, 28% choose Sears as the store they feel least represents their values and another 25% reject Neiman Marcus.

Oh, those Outsiders. Only 29% care at all about locally produced food – the lowest of any tribe by far. The same with the only 40% who say they care about nutritional data (59% do not!) and 41% who pay attention to GMOs (somewhere in the low middle among the tribes). The 49% who are at least somewhat concerned about the environmental impact of food production is near the bottom.

This tribe is small but very real. They rank the lowest or near the lowest on every attribute. Every one. Or since we are going down that road, in the immortal words of Frank Zappa and The Mothers of Invention, "Nothing, not a Goddamned Thing".

This is not a fun group at all. They place the lowest or near lowest value on almost every attribute tested. So to make sure we are all on the same page: they have little need for God, perseverance, fun, moderation, adventure, authenticity, duty, simplicity, optimism or even family.

When it comes to strengthening tribal bonds, we will not see them in church, at a music festival, on a group vacation or a spiritual retreat, a dinner party, tailgating, at their kids' events, at a farmers' market or on Facebook. They are either the lowest or second lowest on all of these.

Almost half (48%) say they are individualists – by far the leader in this category—and 13% see themselves writing the great American novel (second highest).

But back to the "I don't cares", a list which includes real love, true friendship, a loving family, genuine respect, carefree fun, and a life full of meaning. They are the lowest on each of these, except one where they are a close second. They also give the lowest ratings on satisfaction from family vacations or meals, shopping for clothes, being alone with a spouse or friend, on the job, or finding work fulfilling.

Guys of the world: the Outsiders are women (56%). A majority (52%) earn less than $35,000 – by far the most of any tribe. They are less likely to be Born Again or to own their own home. They do have kids at home. They are among the most likely to say they are citizens of their own town—not the United States or the planet Earth -- and they do not support either the Tea Party or Occupy Wall Street. The Outsiders have the highest percentage of non-heterosexuals, people who have lost a job in the past year (15%), fear losing a job in the next year (24%), work at a job that pays less than a previous job (30%), and no religious affiliation. Two in three, among the most of any tribe, have no college experience.

They also have the highest percentage that identify themselves as LGBT.

They hate high school sports (54%), and are least likely to value exercise (43%), eat healthy food (53%), follow politics (13%), or place great value in the American flag (43%).

So what do they like? One in three (33%, higher than any tribe) really feel that celebrity gossip is important. *(Author's Note: She's sitting at the end of the bar – alone, of course).*

THE OUTSIDERS IN THEIR OWN WORDS

One woman described herself as a conservative and said her motto was just "one day at a time". When asked the most important task she would like to complete before she died, she replied only that "I don't have a bucket list". Her definition of success was "being happy" but emphasized that she was not happy.

Another pretty cynical respondent called himself a progressive but said his only motto was "survive", the two most important or life-changing moments in his life were "being born and dying". He would, however, like "to save someone's life" before he dies.

"Just a boring everyday life for me", said one woman. She would like to be "as successful and loved as possible" before she dies, but doubted it would happen.

10. THE DUTIFULS – 26.9% OF ADULTS.

The Z-File On the Dutifuls – All for one and one for all, their connection is that they are honorable, responsible, monogamous, loyal. Straight as an arrow, devoted to traditional values, God-fearing, they have little time for fun. Family is supreme and they are unpretentious. They are the bedrock of an older America and the traditional, Establishment GOP. Eighty percent feel the American flag is very important to them – second among the tribes.

Faith and God are very important to the Dutifuls (73%, second only to the God Squad) but it is their quest for authenticity (92%) and duty/honor (85%) that sets them apart. They also place a premium on simplicity (67%, second place among tribes). They rank number three on family first for themselves and first on the importance of family in their fellow tribesmen.

No tribe sees themselves more as "honorable and trustworthy" as the Dutifuls (37%) or as "compassionate, generous, and accommodating to others" (31%). The 23% who say their lives are best defined as "purposeful and meaningful" rank number one. They see themselves as considerably more "open-minded and balanced" (24%) than other traditional values tribes as the God Squad or the Land of the Free.

This is a conservative-leaning group – 47% are conservative and only 17% are liberal. They have among the higher concentrations of full-time conservatives (27%), with 11% conservative on spending and 8% on social issues. Only 6% are liberal all the time and just 2% are liberal on spending, 9% on social issues. Less than one in four (23%) are moderates.

The Dutifuls always play by the rules. They are not rebellious or in-your-face as the Land of the Free, nor as rigid as the God Squad. They will "go with the flow" but they are not as liberal or zen-like as that tribe.

They are good people. I hesitate to use the word "ordinary" because I hate that description – but they live simply and do what they are sup-posed to do. You won't find them holding up the line at the convenience store to scratch off lottery tickets, nor will you find them standing out in church with the supercilious look that says "I am saved and you are not, you poor schmuck". For them the Good Book is just that – the Good Book – meaning live quietly, follow the Lord, and play by the Golden Rule. Always remember this: a Dutiful will never try to park in a handi-capped space. A God Squad member may say that "I tithe and believe in the will of the Lord, so I am entitled"; a One True Path may argue that "I try to be good and sensitive to others in every way"; a Land of the Free might say "this is a free country so this law is bull", and an Outsider will just say something she shouldn't really say – but a Dutiful will obey the law.

By far, more than any other tribe, they describe the meaning of their life to be "compassionate, generous, accommodating to others" and "honorable and trustworthy".

THE **DUTIFULS**

26.9% OF ADULTS

LIFE MISSION/ MEANING

To live a life that is authentic, one of duty to a higher authority, family-oriented

FACTORS IN CHOOSING FELLOW TRIBE MEMBERS

Immediate family and family-oriented, authenticity, and faith in God

DEFINITION OF SUCCESS

Achieving a loving family

ONE THING MISSING TO COMPLETE LIFE

War heroism, selfless missionary, finding a cure for cancer

STRENGTHENING TRIBAL BONDS

Family vacation, attending a place of worship

DEMOGRAPHICS

Gender Women outnumber men 56% to 44%.

Income Forty-three percent earn under $50,000 and 35% make $50,000-$100,00. Only 23% make over $100,000.

Residence They have the highest concentration of suburbanites (38%), then 20%-22% are found in big cities, small cities, and rural areas. Only 71% own their homes, tied for lowest.

Religion Three in five (61%) are Protestant, the second highest, while 24% are Catholic, 13% nonaffiliated and 3% are Jewish. Thirty-two percent (third highest) attend services at least weekly. Thirty-two percent (third highest) attend services at least weekly but there are 49% who rarely or never do. The 46% who are Born Again are among the highest.

Race/Ethnicity At 78% white they are second only to the Land of the Free, and have the lowest number of Hispanics (7%). There are 10% African American and 3% Asian.

Family They are married (61%, number one of all the tribes), while 19% each are either never married or divorced/separated.

Age **They have the highest concentration of Boomers (32%) and another 25% are over 65. But 43% are under 50.**

Employment Not quite half are working (45%) but 20% are retired. They have the second lowest percentage (9%) of members who have lost a job in the past year due to corporate downsizing and 20% who are working a job that pays less (about average).

Lifestyle Only 16% like NASCAR, 25% identify with the Investor Class, and 31% with the Creative Class. Only 31% are social networkers. Almost half (40%) have a passport.

 POLITICS

Their party affiliation is evenly spread: 33% Democrat, 34% Republican, and 33% independent – but their hearts and minds are clearly conservative (47%). Only 17% are liberal and 35% moderate. One in four (27%) support the Tea Party and only 16% sympathize with Occupy Wall Street.

Like the Outsiders, the Dutifuls have 45% in their ranks who favor neither the Obamas' nor the Pauls' versions of American – the highest numbers of rejectionists. Otherwise, the Dutifuls have another 30% who tilt toward the Pauls and 25% who prefer the Obamas.

This conservative-leaning group does indeed worry about debt with 67% (the third highest) saying government is leading Americans down the path to serfdom and only 20% (second lowest) agreeing that government is a force for good.

About half (48%) are pro-life, but 40% are pro-choice.

Only 37% follow politics closely and 36% say local government is important to them.

Yet the Dutifuls still ended up voting for the re-election of President Obama in 2012 -- 50% to 48%.

🛒 HABITS AND ATTITUDES

The Dutifuls opt for familiarity, security, and safety. They are tied with the God Squad in their desire to shop at Kohl's (17%), though Target is their number store (23%). On the other end of the spectrum come stores that offer more financial insecurity and a social status that is just not them – Neiman Marcus (34%) and Bloomingdales (21%).

While 68% of this tribe pay attention to nutritional data (among the highest), only 35% pay any attention to the use of GMOs (second lowest). Almost half (48%) prefer to locally produced food (50% do not), but only 44% even bother with the environmental impact (the lowest).

While they rank going to a place of worship as very important in strengthening tribal bonds (62%, second to the God Squad), they rate other offerings either low or the lowest – a music festival, tailgating, and farmers' market. They get little satisfaction from shopping for clothes but they are very high on family vacations (81%, actually the highest of any tribe). A majority (56%) would spend a sudden check for $5,000 on their family and friends – more than any other tribe. An equal percentage feel guilty spending less than $100 on themselves.

More than any other tribe, 52% say they have already achieved a loving family. The same with the 43% who have already achieved genuine respect (number one) and the 30% who have already achieved a life full of meaning (number one).

They are more inclined to be concerned about products made in America (62%) than their environmental impact or the type of labor used to produce them.

Their fantasy home is where they currently live (32%, tied for second), but a healthy 27% would not mind that Mediterranean villa (which they could share with the God Squad, with whom they tie).

They are the real patriots – 49% are most inclined to call themselves "American citizens" (the highest of any tribe) as opposed to "residents of their town or city" or "citizens of the planet earth". The Dutifuls are tied for the lowest concentration of under 30 year olds (12%) and the highest concentration of heterosexuals (95%, tied for first).

THE DUTIFULS IN THEIR OWN WORDS

The responses from The Dutifuls revealed a tribe grounded in basic values, no overblown sense of entitlement or ambition beyond their reach, and without any pretense at all. Julie from Southeastern Wisconsin summed her life (and her tribe) perfectly when she described her life: "I met my husband over 36 years ago. We have been a couple for 32 years and married for almost 30. We do our best every day to treat people politely, at the very minimum, and to enjoy each day". In essence that is her motto, too: "Doing the very best I can every day. Make sure I treat people the way I want to be treated". When it comes to choosing friends, she had a different take. "I don't chose friends; they eventually just happen. However, if they aren't good people, I won't be friends with them". And the most important task she would like to complete is "to make sure I have done the best I can every day in how I treat people and make sure everything is set up for our children".

Cheryl from Las Vegas, Nevada, told us "I feel fairly ordinary". A liberal, her motto is "stay hopeful" and her definition of success is "being happy with yourself". Tom from New York City is driven only by the words "keep is simple stupid". His life-changing events include both heart surgery and homelessness, but his one big task to complete is to "write a book". And Brian from near Toledo, Ohio would like to "coach a State champion team" and believes he can do it – yet he chooses his friends on the basis of whether they "humble, down to earth".

"Believe in God" and live life honestly and simply" are what drives a woman respondent. The same holds true for the woman who wrote that her motto is "being true to myself and God, and living responsibly". A devout Muslim, she told us that her "divorce and disability status taught me to not take life for granted and learn to be helpful as a way of giving back and reaching my spiritual side". Her most important task to complete? "Make my pilgrimage to Mecca in Saudi Arabia so I can be a better Muslim and child of God".

The mother of a special needs child wrote that her driving force in life is to be a "good parent" and her most important task remains to "make sure my children will be okay after I die". Others kept it just as simple for mottos and tasks: "family", "enough money for family", "get life insurance", "always be honest, faithful and forgiving, "assure that my family is well taken care of", "just thankful to be alive".

11. THE CREATORS – 14.5% OF ADULTS.

The Z-File On the Creators – They are inner-directed, dance to their own drumbeat, and are always willing to use their creativity and ingenuity to make the future they want. They are the free spirits and are inner directed, artsy, romantic. The Creators are certainly not brooding loners nor hostile iconoclasts. Rather, they appear to be well adjusted and happy.

What are they in a phrase? They say they are best described as "creative and enriched" (26%), a percentage that is double digits higher than that of the Adventurists and Happy Hedonists (15% and 14% respectively). They also see themselves as "determined, persistent, and overcoming" (24%) and "open-minded and balanced" (24%).

While they certainly identify much more with the America of the Obamas than that of the Pauls, this tribe is about evenly-spread ideologically. Almost one in three (30%) describe themselves as liberals – 15% all the time, and 8% each fiscally and socially. Twenty-nine percent are conservative (22% all the time and only 3% fiscally and 4% soically). And 41% are moderates.

There is clearly an attitude here. More than two times that of any other tribe this tribe's members describe themselves as "creative and enriched" and they are at the top in calling themselves a "work in progress". But their consideration of being that work in progress is far different than the Persistents who fight to survive, to maintain, to swim. The Creators strive for greatness, to be triumphant, for individual glory. Regardless of where they live physically, their minds and hearts belong on the Upper East Side.

THE CREATORS

14.5% OF ADULTS

LIFE MISSION/ MEANING

To be rebellious, adventurous, authentic

FACTORS IN CHOOSING FELLOW TRIBE MEMBERS

Authentic, honest, adventurous, and optimistic

DEFINITION OF SUCCESS

Freedom to pursue own passion, be own person, define own success

ONE THING MISSING TO COMPLETE LIFE

Write the great American novel and star in a movie

STRENGTHENING TRIBAL BONDS

Attend a music festival, group vacation, spiritual retreat

 **DEMOGRAPHICS**

Gender 54% women, 46% men.

Income 50% earn under $50,000, 28% earn $50,000-$100,000, and 22% over $100,000.

Residence 27% in large cities (on the high side), 24% in small cities, 32% suburbs, and 17% rural. Sixty-six percent own their homes.

Religion The 26% who are nonaffiliated are among the highest among the tribes, and the 44% Protestants are well below average followed by the 26% Catholics who are average. The 5% who are Jewish is the highest concentration. Thirty-nine percent of the small number of Protestants are Born Again and 57% of the total rarely/never attend religious services.

Family While 46% are married, 30% are single/never married, and 19% are divorced/separated (tied for highest).

Race/Ethnicity They have a lower percentage of whites (68%), while 16% are Hispanic, 10% African American, and 4% Asian.

Age Fifty-eight percent are under 50 – 24% 18-19, 34% 30-49. One in four (27%) are 50-64 and 15% over 65.

Employment A little more than half (52%) are working and only 12% are retired, while 20% fear losing their job and 18% are working for less. At 38% they are the third highest in considering their current employment "a gig".

Lifestyle They have a fairly high percentage of social networkers (38%), 44% have passports, 24% are in the Investor Class, and 23%

shop at least weekly at Wal-Mart, and 42% (tied for highest of any tribe) are in the Creative Class. Three in five (61%) have at least a college degree.

 ## POLITICS

The Creators are Democrats (42% to only 16% Republicans and 29% independents). And 30% are liberals, the same as those who are conservatives. Two in five (41%) are moderates. Only 15% sympathize with the Tea Party (the lowest) while 19% support Occupy Wall Street.

By a 15 point margin, the Creators identify with the America of the Obamas (42% to 25%), yet by 16 points (48% to 32%) they fear the lack of sustainability of government spending forcing Americans down the path to serfdom.

But 49% are pro-choice and only 31% are pro-life.

They talk liberal and they vote liberal. In 2012 they supported the President in his re-election bid 69% to 28%.

 ## HABITS AND ATTITUDES

Nothing really creative here. Target is tops (22%), followed by Macy's (13%) and Kohl's (12%), and Wal-Mart (14%). The Creators also just do not get Neiman Marcus (26%).

Author Daniel Pink (*A Whole New Mind: Why Right Brainers Will Rule the Future*) suggests that the future may very well belong to the right brain. It could also be because the Creators tribe pays closest attention to the food they eat and, thus, they will live longer. More than any other tribe, 77% of the Creators scrutinize labels for nutritional data, 68% pay heed to locally produced food, and 64% care about the environmental safety of contents of the food they buy (second highest). The 47% who follow closely GMO use place this tribe in third place in that category.

The Creators love life and want to do big things, but mainly on their own terms. They are kindred spirits with Happy Hedonists and Adventurists, rating just below these tribes in being adventurous and rebellious. They rank third in seeking balance/zen in their lives.

Not surprisingly, they are more likely to find them at music festivals (70%, by far the highest who say that these strengthen tribal bonds) but they also get a kick out of farmer's markets. (I mean, where else are you likely to find gluten-free-oatmeal/honey soaps and handmade dulcimers?) They rank second among tribes in their desire to be movie stars and third in wanting to write the great American novel.

They rate at the very top or very near the top on achieving life's noblest of goals: real love, true friendship, a loving family, carefree fun, and personal fulfillment. They make a lot of their purchases on the basis of products they perceive to be eco-friendly and human rights-friendly. And they do dress to look attractive.

One in three (32%) love high school sports, more than any other tribe. Four in five (79%) say eating healthy food is very important (the highest) and 21% enjoy celebrity gossip – about their fellow creatives, I suppose.

CREATORS IN THEIR OWN WORDS

Carolyn of Sheboygan, Wisconsin stated her motto and perhaps the anthem of the Creators tribe perfectly: "think outside the box", while Darren from Central Florida said he lives to "work hard and play hard" and the most important task for him to finish is to "see the world". Vonda from Gainesville, Florida didn't disagree. "Shoot for the moon, even if I miss, I'll be among the stars". Even living with poor health and finances, she defined success as "feeling complete and successful".

"Keep on trucking'", said Kathy of Andover, Massachusetts. Her most important task to complete before death is "making a difference and achieving more success by being able to indulge my creativity". So what is success for Kathy? "I am here. It is my turn on the planet. What am I going to do with it?" Walter from Baltimore, Maryland is driven by wanting to "write books all the time" and his most important goal in life is "complete and publish four books with my son as co-author". He told us that he has already "published 24 Kindle eBooks and written 50 country western songs" and will have succeeded in life by "having an excellent relationship with my son and continuing to be creative".

While many of the Creators are liberal or progressive, Duane from the Northeast corner of Florida was one of the conservatives. "I am an author trying to make a buck in an industry controlled by publishers who only publish works from celebrities". But for him, the guiding force is "live free or die". Christine, who like Anthony Bourdain is from "parts unknown", said that one of her two life-changing moments was "when I realized what I wanted to do with my life (be a writer". Her one task to complete in life was a tie – "become a published author or own a house of my own (even if it's a mobile)".

One respondent said he is very happy and one his defining moments was when he decided to "go to the school paper to see if they needed a cartoonist and it was there I met my future wife". Success for this artist is "being able to do what I want to do".

TABLES

The following tables are useful in our discussion in the next two chapters on how the tribes are both unique and how they overlap.

WHICH OF THE FOLLOWING BEST DESCRIBES THE ANIMAL YOU REPRESENT?	GWF	HH	GOD	PER	SP	ADV	LOF	OTP	OUT	DUTI	CRE
Solitary Leopard	16	6	10	21	26	6	13	9	15	14	6
Free-Spirited Horse	13	19	12	10	9	17	19	15	8	10	21
Mysterious Chameleon	10	12	6	6	3	10	6	9	7	6	21
Ruthless Crocodile	1	6	1	1	--	4	1	1	6	--	--
Predatory Wolf	3	2	-	1	8	6	2	1	1	--	1
Intelligent Chimp	9	16	14	23	11	20	16	13	8	28	10
Timid Mouse	7	2	6	12	17	1	2	6	14	6	7
Insignificant Amoeba	1	1	1	--	--	3	2	3	7	3	1
Sociable Zebra	10	10	17	11	7	11	14	13	12	15	7
Legendary Unicorn	7	11	3	3	4	9	5	10	6	5	6

IN YOUR WILDEST DREAMS WHAT ARE YOU DRIVING?	GWF	HH	GOD	PER	SP	ADV	LOF	OTP	OUT	DUTI	CRE
Sports Car	8	13	13	14	4	22	16	14	8	15	11
Luxury Car	13	14	14	16	11	25	14	16	11	22	25
SUV	18	24	27	27	28	28	24	18	25	23	16
Hybrid	18	15	8	12	23	4	9	6	18	10	7
Just a Car	32	31	33	29	19	18	30	37	25	27	30

IN YOUR WILDEST DREAMS WHERE ARE YOU LIVING?

	GWF	HH	GOD	PER	SP	ADV	LOF	OTP	OUT	DUTI	CRE
Medieval Castle in Europe	4	13	6	13	6	16	11	11	19	7	6
Mediterranean Villa	28	27	19	32	35	24	24	22	7	28	30
Beverly Hills Mansion	10	22	7	5	13	15	6	9	20	5	11
Colorado Ski Lodge	3	6	4	6	7	6	3	13	5	5	4
New York City Penthouse	7	3	7	6	23	15	12	5	6	4	5
Current Home	28	23	39	25	13	17	32	36	21	34	33

IN YOUR WILDEST DREAMS WHAT ARE PEOPLE SAYING ABOUT YOU?

	GWF	HH	GOD	PER	SP	ADV	LOF	OTP	OUT	DUTI	CRE
You are the... person											
Richest	12	11	5	14	4	23	12	13	3	11	9
Prettiest	7	18	7	8	16	17	5	6	16	3	4
Smartest	32	26	23	40	32	39	31	29	22	32	49
Funniest	28	38	26	18	24	39	27	33	34	21	43
Nicest	62	48	70	60	51	42	61	61	51	66	59
Thinnest	3	6	2	6	2	6	3	2	1	3	5
Happiest	52	51	53	53	56	42	52	47	18	49	50
Luckiest	25	23	23	37	18	21	25	19	29	24	21

HAVE GONE WITHOUT FOOD FOR 24 HOURS IN THE PAST MONTH DUE TO LACK OF MONEY OR FOOD?

	GWF	HH	GOD	PER	SP	ADV	LOF	OTP	OUT	DUTI	CRE
Yes	16	17	15	14	10	17	10	11	21	13	9

IN MY OPINION THE AMERICAN DREAM IS

	GWF	HH	GOD	PER	SP	ADV	LOF	OTP	OUT	DUTI	CRE
Alive and well	34	53	32	31	35	42	29	43	18	33	40
Barely breathing	42	35	48	56	45	52	58	45	47	55	41
Dead	11	9	12	8	8	4	4	9	31	6	7

WHICH OF THE FOLLOWING DOLLAR FIGURES REPRESENTS HOW MUCH YOU CAN SPEND ON YOURSELF WITHOUT FEELING GUILTY?

	GWF	HH	GOD	PER	SP	ADV	LOF	OTP	OUT	DUTI	CRE
Less than $100	43	37	62	50	53	45	53	42	61	61	51
$101-$500	24	28	20	29	3	22	20	18	13	19	16
$501-$1000	9	10	4	4	11	7	8	14	3	8	8
$1000-$5000	5	8	2	5	--	13	5	4	--	3	1
$5000 or more	12	21	7	8	10	9	7	13	4	6	9

CHAPTER 3

WE ARE MANY: TRIBAL
UNIQUENESS AND DISSONANCE

People are different and seek out others who help give shape to their own identities. We now have greater capacity to do that for ourselves without having to wait to meet the person in history class, the co-worker sitting on a bench, or the video dating site. You can't have a melting pot without diversity and we now have many more ways to obtain diverse people with varying interests. And there are many more ways for them to communicate with each other and express their own unique characteristics, talents, ideas, hobbies, and habits. Every tribe has its persons of color, its young and old and in between ages, its Easterners or Southerners, its NBA fans and its gardening enthusiasts. And each tribe has its own biases and political positions. At the same time we know the power of being in a group of peers. Journalist Tina Rosenberg's *Join the Club* has documented how vital the opinions and values of peers can be in not only influencing the behavior of the individual but also on the collective of the peer group. From peer review committees who decide who will receive microloans and monitor the behavior of recipients to kitchen table counseling sessions to decisions among young women whether or not they should have sex, the role of peers plays a major role in our lives.

Importantly, in the Zogby Analytics open-ended surveys, Americans actually got to name their own tribes in addition to identifying the attributes that describe and offer most meaning to their lives. As the tribes formed early in the survey process, and were validated and shaped in subsequent surveys, distinct differences clearly emerged. The following table highlights only a few of these characteristics that make each tribe a separate entity – the ranking of priority values.

TRIBAL CONTRASTS
RANKING OF CHARACTERISTICS BY TRIBE

VERY IMPORTANT	GWF	HH	GOD	PER	SP	ADV	LOF	OTP	OUT	DUTI	CRE
Attending Place of Worship	6	5	1	3	6	7	7	2	9	4	8
First In Neighborhood to Try a New Product	2	1	5	8	2	3	9	7	4	10	6
The American Flag	7	8	1	4	8	6	2	5	9	3	10
Celebrity Gossip	2	1	5	6	3	3	7	5	4	8	8
Traditional Marriage Between Man and Woman Only	6	7	1	5	5	8	3	2	6	4	9

In this section, I will take an even closer look at each of the 11 tribes and note what makes each different, a stand alone. For marketers, communications professionals, political strategists, community organizers – i.e. those whose business it is to reach, influence, and mobilize people –

here, I hope, is a guide to how best to deal with each tribe once they are identified in your base of customers, voters, even friends. For you who may not be in any of these kinds of professions, here is a way to understand those who are in (or not in) your own tribe a tad better.

The God Squad has by far the highest correlation with the attribute "love of God, my faith" as they are basically an unpretentious lot, meaning that they for the most part eschew bigger cars or homes, or wildest fantasies. Their lives center around family and, at least in a material sense, the cards they have been dealt. As for the future, that all seems to be in the hands of God.

Stated simply, the best approach to the God Squad is through their faith, which illuminates how they live.

Values and Attributes **This tribe's members give lowest priority to "living it up and having fun" and (along with The Dutifuls) are least likely to "seek balance and go with the flow".** To God Squadders, being "rebellious" is least important and they also reject more than any tribe "material pleasures and owning possessions" as a life priority. They place their greatest emphasis on "duty, responsibility, honor and courage" and they are truly inspired by their faith because of all the tribes, they are among the most "optimistic and inspired". Accurately reflecting their conservative ideology and biases, they think that America is headed down the wrong track (58%) and 80% say the future of the American Dream is not so bright. They are a self-reliant bunch, not particularly trusting in the nation's leadership. Three of four, among the most of any tribe, give highest priority to overcoming odds. This and the afterlife are matters that involve themselves and a Higher Being.

While a majority identify with the "adventurous/seeking new challenges", they are certainly nowhere near the level of the "Happy Hedonists" and "Adventurists". Which attributes best define their lives? "Blessed and saved" is the top choice (49%), followed by "honorable and trustworthy" (36%) and "compassionate and generous" (35%). They told us the top two behaviors that strengthen their tribe's bonds are "attendance at a place of worship" (85%), a "spiritual retreat" (72%) and going to kids' school events (68%). No arrogance here: they are the "sociable zebra" and "Homey Earth", when we asked which best describes who they really are.

They are not and will not be conspicuous spenders. Grandiose appeals and promises, luxury dream vacations, and the lure of material acquisitions are simply not what the members of the God Squad are all about. Sixty-two percent feel guilty spending less than $100 on themselves, and huge numbers are happiest when eating a normal family meal and alone reading a good book. **Perhaps, it can be argued, that they are thrifty because 75% of this tribe have household incomes of less than $75,000.** They also tend to be older and thus less "burdened" with heavier responsibilities than tribes that have a larger portion of younger folks. In either case, their expectations are basic for this life and it will be difficult to lead them with wild fantasy-based messaging or promises of an extravagant, over-the-top kind of life that they just do not want.

Nine in ten say that a "place of worship" is most/very important to them, the highest of any tribe. Three in four, high but not the highest, say the same about the American flag.

Who is favored to play the life (or leading man) in the movie about a God Squad-er? Mel Gibson is first (17%), followed by Tom Hanks (16%), Matt Damon (15%), and Jamie Foxx (13%). Tops for leading lady? Clearly, Julia Roberts (26%) and Halle Barry (13%). Mel Gibson represents – at least more than anyone else listed as a choice in the survey – fundamental Christianity and old-fashioned conservativism (including some pretty base elements of anti-Semitism). Tom Hanks is Hollywood's "Mr. Nice Guy" – and also a hero to older Americans for his stunning role in *Saving Private Ryan.* Julia Roberts is "America's Sweetheart", a young glamorous actress who has segued nicely into her role in real life as a traditional Mom.

As consumers the God Squad is thrifty and no frills. Half say they do care about whether a product is environmentally friendly or violates the rights of workers, but two of three say that "Made in America" is of high concern. Zogby polling over the past decade has discovered a growing sensibility regarding the environment and global human rights. While self-described liberals show greater concern for these issues, it is a mistake to characterize these issues in the context of a liberal-conservative debate. We have heard terms like "man's stewardship of God's earth" and "Christian concern for the treatment of workers" among those who define themselves as fundamentalist. At the same time, in keeping with the "neo-tribe" paradigm, liberals and moderates can certainly fit into the God Squad. And the God Squad includes 60% women – very possibly a factor in identifying with the environment and human rights. Nonetheless, members of the God Squad are more likely to identify with patriotism. And in keeping with their simple tastes, only one in four prefer the Tiffany label over a much lower-cost version of a product in a Wal-Mart bag; only 15% say it is important to look of a higher class than they are. Not surprisingly, Wal-Mart is among their favorite stores.

What are they driving in their wildest fantasy? "Just my own car" say 33%, more than any other tribe. And 40% are living "in their current home", instead of a luxury mansion, a chalet in the Swiss Alps, or Mediterranean villa—again higher than any other tribe. They want people to say they are the "nicest person" (70%, higher than any other tribe) and have the lowest percentage of any tribe who want people to say they are the "smartest" (23%) or the "richest" (5%). Interestingly, two in five (as we will see below) say that "continuing learning…staying intellectually challenged" is very important to them. But it appears that the knowledge attained is not the type that empowers this tribe's members to fly too close to the sun. One in four says that their current income or less is enough to make them happy.

Land of the Free is the largest tribe. They represent an amalgam of the most traditional values: duty and responsibility, perseverance, simplicity, and optimism. Three in four place love of God and faith as highest priority – which is high, but not as high the God Squad. On the low end of their priorities are having fun (43%), rebelliousness/defiance (23%), and materialism/owning possessions (26%). The top three characteristics that describe their lives are honorable/trustworthy (39%), blessed/saved (28%), and trustworthy/hard work (28%).

Their religious faith is important but not as intense as that of the God Squad. The LOF cite going to a school event for their kids and attending a place of worship as the top ritual/behaviors that strengthen their tribal bonds (68% and 63% respectively), followed by going on a group vacation (54%) or a religious retreat (54%).

Spunkier than the God Squad, 19% identify with the free-spirited horse – the second highest of any tribe. At the same time, 66% of the Land Of the Free feel that the American Dream is either dead or barely breathing, the highest of any tribe and about half (48%) say the American Dream's future is not bright, the most of any tribe. Zogby polling has shown that the American Dream itself is under major reconstruction in a number of ways. Through thick and thin, three in four Americans would always say that the Dream was alive, well and achievable. By the beginning of the new Millennium, we had seen a steady shift in redefining the American Dream in more spiritual and less material terms. But as the Great Recession hit later in the decade, confidence in the American Dream waned and an entirely new factor arose that has actually dominated the discussion (actually ALL discussions) – hyper-partisanship. Hence, if you are a Republican and/or self-described conservative under President Barack Obama, you are much more likely to feel that the American Dream, the direction of the country, and the nation's future are doing poorly. This is regardless of whether your income has risen, you have received a job promotion, or other objective criteria are sufficiently high. (And the same holds true if you are a Democrat, liberal, or are one of the key demographic groups that supported Mr. Obama's election or re-election even if you have lost ground or are doing poorly financially, you are much more likely to feel the American Dream is alive). Thus, in this context, it is not surprising that members of the Land of the Free – an otherwise vibrant and lively group – would say they are pessimistic.

After the God Squad, they have the highest percentage who attends religious services weekly or more at a place of worship.

While considering the environmental friendliness or the labor practices involved in a product are not unimportant, patriotism (Made in America) is the chief concern – 82% say it is important, more than any other tribe. The LOF also place more emphasis on looking attractive (63%) and they do better with fantasies than the God Squad – 18% are driving a sports car in their wildest dreams – although one in three are still living in their current home (rejecting a Mediterranean villa and a Beverly Hills mansion). They also prefer being seen as nice and happy.

More than any other tribe, this group prefers Wal-Mart as their favorite store and 42% say they can be happy living on 20% higher than their current income or less. Three in four prioritize eating healthy food, relatively high among the tribes.

And while the hero of the God Squad is the selfless missionary, the LOF most identify with the war hero who saved lives. They are feisty, ready to preserve their older, whiter, heterosexual America. Their belief that the American Dream is on life support starts with the recognition that an African American is now President of their United States, especially one that embodies what they feel is stealing their America away from them right before their very eyes. Tip O'Neill famously said, "All politics is local". To the Land of the Free all life is local.

The Happy Hedonists is a small group and is all about seeking and having fun.

The Happy Hedonists are singularly characterized by their optimism – 90% place highest priority on being optimistic. Seven in ten say they are adventurous. They have high percentages that focus on material possessions (60% define their American Dream as "having money in the bank", far and away more than any other tribe) and are rebellious (38%), which is higher than most tribes). But 68% give high priority to love of God and their faith and the top three values that describe their lives are "hard work" (35%), "relaxed" (33%) and "compassion" (29%). They appear to be quite comfortable in their own shoes.

What strengthens their tribal bonds? Taking a group vacation is first (85%) and they rank highest among the tribes in getting group strength from a tailgating party (55%), walking along a farmers' market (41%), and chatting online (42%). While a majority place high value on attending a spiritual retreat, only 37% draw strength from attending a place of worship (the lowest of any tribe).

This tribe includes people who feel awfully good about themselves – 16% identify as being an intelligent chimpanzee (the highest), 11% a legendary unicorn and 20% say they are mysterious Venus (both the second highest of tribes). For this tribe, the American Dream is alive and well (53%, the highest) and they identify that dream as "money in the bank" (the highest). Two in three (66%) say the future of the Dream is bright.

They, in keeping with their name, live for the moment: 29% -- the highest among tribes -- can spend $1,000 or more on themselves before they start feeling guilty. While the American flag is important to Happy Hedonists (64%), church attendance is not (only 46%). More than any other tribe, 24% say that celebrity gossip is important to them.

They may be self-centered, but they are not selfish. As consumers, more of this tribe care deeply about consumer products that are environmentally friendly (58%) and the labor practices involved in production

(62%). Made in America is a consideration to 59%. More than any other tribe, 44% of the Happy Hedonists say it is important to look of a higher class than they are and 75% say it is most important to show that "you are yourself".

They are neither the God Squad nor the Land of the Free when it comes to fantasies.

Where are they living? One in five (26%) are in a Beverly Hills mansion and 13% in a castle in Europe – both the highest of any tribe. Hedonists to the bone, 55% say people are saying that others are most likely saying about them that they are the happiest, 46% the funniest, and 26% the prettiest – all the highest. (When they wake up, they still feel people are saying they are the funniest and happiest).

How much money do they need to make them happy? More than any other tribe, 57% say they need twice their current income while only 19% can hack it on 20% more than their current income or less – the highest and the lowest. How about just to live comfortably? Forty-four percent say they need twice their current income or more. (They are Hedonists, after all).

While 77% have shopped at a dollar store hey, you have to trade down to be able to occasionally trade up -- that is the lowest of any tribe. Forty-five percent say it is important to be the first in their neighborhood to try a new product (highest) and 29% have always wanted a luxury car (the highest).

One in five (19%) choose the war hero as their own hero and another 18% pick the self-made billionaire. And their leading man in the movie about themselves? Leonardo DiCaprio (30% the highest), then Matt Damon (17%) and Eddie Murphy (14%). The leading lady is Halle Barry with 26%, then Julia Roberts (17%) and Natalie Portman (12%). In other words, they opt for manly men and pretty women.

The Happy Hedonists are not all young but they are young at heart. And for them, in the words of Frank Sinatra, "fairy tales can come true, they can happen to you, if you're young at heart." They seek and embody the joys of life.

The Adventurists is the tribe whose members see themselves driven by adventure, rebellion, and material pleasures.

There is little equivocation from this tribe as to what is most important. Nine in ten describe themselves as adventurous and welcoming new challenges and optimistic and happy. Seven in ten prioritize efforts to seek and have fun. Two of three emphasize material possessions and 43% are rebellious (the highest of any tribe). More than any other tribe they say they are open-minded (32%).

A majority (56%) say that attending a spiritual retreat strengthens their tribal binds, but that places them somewhere in the middle among other tribes. They are low, however, bonding over church attendance. **Not surprisingly, they are high on tailgating and local sports. More than any other tribe, 40% bond over attending a farmers' market.** Adventurists seem to be driven by the need to travel – seeking the next gig, pursuing the exotic new experience, or to simply "finding themselves". There is a fairly high a (though not dominant) concentration of "First Globals" (18-36 year olds) in this tribe so that means a combination of the Wanderlust of youth but also that this is a group who already has the world at its fingertips and wants to see and feel as much of it in their lifetime as possible.

Forty-five percent (more than any of the other tribes) describe themselves as individualists, 20% as an intelligent chimpanzee, 17% a free-spirited horse (both on the high side among tribes), and they are tops in their goal to explore the bottom of the ocean (16%) and saying they resemble very hot Mercury (10%). In short, this is a tribe where its members feel very good about themselves and their own future. They are, as we have seen already, different demographically and politically from the Happy Hedonists.

The Adventurists also are great believers in the American Dream. More than any tribe, they wholeheartedly believe in it (55%), are actively pursuing it (63%), and are spending more time on it (63%). A majority (51%, more than others) define it as the freedom to pursue their own passions and 62% say the future of the American Dream looks bright. This tribe still believes in the American Dream and that is a positive sign for the nation.

They are least satisfied of any tribe reading a good book (35%), at a typical family meal (36%), and watching television alone (2%) – but most satisfied shopping for clothes for themselves. More than any other tribe, 27% of the Adventurists can spend $5000 on themselves without feeling guilty.

Regular exercise tops the list of what is most important to them (84%), followed by eating healthy (82%). Seven in ten say the American flag is important and 56% prioritize local government, the most of any tribe.

One in five (18%) are into celebrity gossip – high, but not as high as the Hedonists.

Their runaway top choice for leading man to play them is Matt Damon (26%), followed by Leonardo DiCaprio (15%) and Tom Cruise (10%). Halle Barry is the top leading lady with 27% (more than any other tribe), followed by young Emma Watson (21%) and not so young Julia Roberts (21%). More than any other tribe, 47% of Adventurers choose a war hero as their main hero.

The Adventurists care more than any other tribes about environmentally friendly products (61%) and are most concerned about labor practices. They are also high on Made in America products (68%). Even more than the Happy Hedonists, they see looking attractive as important (82%), want to appear to be of a higher class (45%), and don't care what anyone thinks (45%). But they also prioritize the need to look all business (45%) more than any other tribe.

Their fantasy car is an SUV (28%), but more than any other tribe they are dreaming about driving a either a luxury car (25%) or a sports car (22%). Less than any tribe they are driving their current car in their fantasies (18%). There is no modesty about choosing the home of their dreams: 24% are in a Beverly Hills mansion or a castle in Europe (16%). Only 17% prefer their current home – second lowest. They want others to say they are the funniest person in both their dreams and in real life.

Just like the Happy Hedonists, 56% of the Adventurers say they need at least twice their current income to be happy. Their number one store is Target (26%) but 83% have shopped at a dollar store. Half need to be the first in their neighborhood to try a new product and one in four (23%) have always wanted a second home – both first among tribes.

Experience tops stuff. They want to do it all and see it all. They are mobile, sensual, confident, but grounded. They are – unlike the God Squad and the Land of the Free – optimistic.

The Go With the Flow Zen and balance define this tribe.

This tribe's members lead all others in identifying themselves as open-minded and balanced (35%) and as a work in progress (32%). They are the folks most likely to call themselves mysterious Venus (21%) while 16% say they are the solitary leopard – the highest. Living a life full of meaning (69%) and personal fulfillment (66%) dominate the description of their lives, as does finding real love (54%) and genuine respect for others (53%, the highest of all tribes). They find solitary experiences most satisfying – reading a book alone (54%) and being alone with a spouse (52%). What strengthens their tribal bonds? Attending a spiritual retreat (41%) and attending a local sports event (42%). "Still waters run deep", according to the old Latin proverb.

As consumers, when it comes to caring about environmentally friendly and fair trade practices, the Go With the Flows pretty much go with the flow – about average. **They fantasize about being the nicest person (62%, third highest) and need less income than any group to be comfortable.** Their fantasy car is more likely to be a hybrid (18%, second highest) than any other car, but they dream about living in a Mediterranean villa more than any other tribe (27%). (May the Flow be with you!) At first glance, it would appear that there is a direct correlation between lower level of income and a lack of material pursuit and fantasy. That could be true to a certain degree. More and more Americans are working at jobs that pay less and (combined with a more general decline in purchasing power among other Americans) they live with an anvil hanging over their head. To be sure, that can dampen the wildest dreams. At the same time, this sentiment of going with the flow has certainly taken on a more spiritual expression – a purposeful reduction of interest in material things. However, one shot at living in a villa does not make a lifestyle – only a whim.

To 42% of the Go With the Flow the American Dream is freedom to pursue their passions – yet they are mainly passionless on most issues. Matt Damon (15%) and Ashton Kutcher (14%) are the top choices to play their life story while Natalie Portman (15%) and Julia Roberts (15%) are the preferred leading ladies.

The Dutifuls is also a modest tribe that treasures authenticity and family in its lives. There is nothing flashy about that. Members of this tribe describe their priorities to include being honorable and trustworthy (43%) and compassionate (42%) – both the highest of any tribe – and hard work (35%). They feel that attending a place of worship strengthens their tribal bond (58%), which is high but nowhere near the God Squad or the Land of the Free. They are neither into tailgating nor farmers' markets. They are least likely to describe themselves as individualists yet they do identify with the intelligent chimp.

They have the least faith in the American Dream: only 33% say it is alive and well, only 27% say it looks bright and 23% spend more time on it, all second lowest. They give the lowest priority scores for achieving real love, obtaining genuine respect from others, having carefree fun, living a life full of meaning, and gaining personal fulfillment. They have a responsibility to their community and that comes first.

"Semper fi" is the rallying cry of the United States Marines and could be the mantra of the **Dutifuls**.

They have the lowest interest in high school sports and local government and are least likely of any tribe to not want to be the first to try a new product (89% lowest score). "Just doing my job, M'am," the immortal words of Sergeant Joe Friday of televisions's *Dragnet*.

A huge 61% of Dutifuls – more than any other tribe – feel guilty spending $100 or less on themselves. They seem less concerned about environmentally friendly products and fair trade practices, just not as much as most tribes. They are the least likely to care what anyone thinks about the way they dress. They want to simply be the nicest person in their fantasies and in reality and in their dreams they are driving their current car. Wal-Mart is their favorite store (26%), followed by Target (23%) and Kohl's (16%) – but none of these numbers is spectacular. Just average folks – they work a lot, are thankful for what they have, and have little focus on or bitterness toward what they do not have and cannot attain. There are no big problems to give them angst.

The Persistents – This tribe sees itself through the prism of dealing with life's struggles, perseverance, and determination to move on. Almost this entire tribe (94%) defines perseverance and overcoming odds as the most important aspect of their lives. Of the attributes that describe their lives, determined and persistent (35% the highest of the tribes), followed by compassionate (33% which is high) and hard work (34% also high).

Second among the Persistents see themselves as the solitary leopard (23%) and mysterious Venus (18%). While they draw tribal strength from both school events (78%) and attendance at a place of worship (69%), this tribe's members find more comfort in spiritual retreats and farmers' markets. They are not inclined to put much faith in the American Dream – only 40% believe in it, which is well below the national average and light years from the 1990s when three in four Americans said it was achievable for most Americans.

They feel their hero is the selfless missionary (38%, the highest of any tribe).

They show more concern for labor practices (62%) than any other tribe and 53% care about environmentally friendly products. Only 6% would choose a similar item in a Tiffany Box over a similar one from Wal-Mart. Their fantasy car is their current car (31%, the highest), but they do dream about a Mediterranean villa (29%). More than any other tribe, they can be happy with 20% more than what they are earning and less. It was stunning for me to see from the early open-ended surveys just how many people have experienced and have lives defined by personal tragedy. **Losing a child, a limb, a relationship, or having bouts with physical or mental illness – these are not single moment traumas. They are lived every day.** This tribe is not about succumbing to or merely surviving pain. They are all about being triumphant in the face of it.

The Self-Perfectionists - This is not a very pleasant tribe to be around. They have the lowest or near lowest ratings on every one of the attributes listed in the survey. While 56% do rate "authenticity/honesty" as most or very important, that is still the lowest of any tribe. They don't even enjoy a trip to the farmers' market, for God's sake. Only one in four

(26%) say they have already achieved true love – by far the lowest.

They are among the least concerned about the environment and human rights when it comes to shopping preferences and near the bottom among tribes that feel that the American Dream is alive and well (35%). Only 26% of the Self-Perfectionists even believe in the American Dream.

More than any other tribe, however, they dream about that Mediterranean villa (35%) and they are at the very top in dreaming about fantasizing about living in a New York City penthouse (23%). One in three want others to think they are the smartest person they know – which is high. One in six hope to write the great American novel – the most of any tribe.

They wouldn't be caught dead in Wal-Mart – only 24% prefer the Arkansas icon. The Happy Hedonists want fun; the Adventurists want life writ large. Together with the ultra-self confident Self-Perfectionists, these are the poster children for Mastercard and American Express – "master the possibilities".

The One True Path – What sets this group apart is their quest for authenticity. Ninety-percent (tied for highest) cite this as the most important attribute. At the same time, they place the highest value on family (91%). This is in sharp contrast with the only 29% high importance on fun. Nine in ten (90%) seek out authenticity in other members of their tribe – both the highest value and the highest of any tribe. They also place a high premium on their fellow tribesmen's simplicity (68%, number one) and perseverance (75%, number one).

The OTP's tribal bonds can be strengthened best at a place of worship

(71%), but they also can be enhanced at a music festival (44%, tied for highest with Happy Hedonists), getting buzzed at a tailgating party (25%, the third highest after the Happy Hedonists and the Adventurists), attending a local sports event , a school event for their children, or on Facebook – all high. They are younger than the God Squad and the Land of the Free and more conservative and serious than the Happy Hedonists and the Adventurists. They include many of the newer face of the young, Christian conservatives – more global, more inclusive, and more socially conscious.

They have more of a positive view of themselves and the American Dream than the other conservative tribes: that 11% aspire to become either President of the United States or the CEO of a company – the most of any tribe. To them the American Dream is very much alive. Forty-three percent say the Dream is alive (second highest), 31% define it as being able to live a better life than their parents (second highest), 35% say it means that they can be their own person (second highest), and 41% wholeheartedly believe in it (high).

This group even finds their job fulfilling – 56%, second highest of any tribe. They also fantasize about living in their current home (second highest) and being the smartest person others know (39%). They aspire to being the first in their neighborhood to try something new (third highest) and they have the second highest percentage of people who prefer Wal-Mart. They barely have any Mac users (.3%, the lowest of any tribe).

They are aspirational and focused. Their eyes are on the prize.

The Outsiders – This is not a fun group at all. They place the lowest or near lowest value on almost every attribute tested. So to make sure we are all on the same page: they have little need for God, perseverance, fun, moderation, adventure, authenticity, duty, simplicity, optimism or even family.

When it comes to strengthening tribal bonds, we will not see them in church, at a music festival, on a group vacation or a spiritual retreat, a dinner party, tailgating, at their kids' events, at a farmers' market or on Facebook. They are either the lowest or second lowest on all of these.

Only 18% feel the American Dream is alive and well – half as many as the next lowest tribe --and only 20% wholeheartedly believe in it. A mere 7% say they are presently living their Dream (second lowest) and only 24% are actively pursuing it (by far the lowest).

Almost 48% say they are individualists – by far the leader in this category—and 13% see themselves writing the great American novel (second highest). They seek comfort alone, but while they achieve the "alone" part, they are hardly comfortable in any way.

But back to the "I don't cares", a list which includes real love, true friendship, a loving family, genuine respect, carefree fun, and a life full of meaning. They are the lowest on each of these, except one where they are a close second. They also give the lowest ratings on satisfaction for family vacations or meals, shopping for clothes, being alone with a spouse or friend, on the job, or finding work fulfilling.

They care little for the environment or human rights (somewhat but low). They can be lonely in a castle in Europe (number one) and in keeping up the iconoclastic image, 21% see the great inventor as their hero. More than any other tribe, 70% listen to FM music in the car – a great way to avoid any news of the world beyond their minds.

The Creators –The Creators love life and want to do big things, but mainly on their own terms. They are kindred spirits with Happy Hedonists and Adventurists, rating just below these tribes in being adventurous and rebellious. They rank third in seeking balance/zen in their lives.

They don't have any wild fantasies beyond the ordinary. But they spend their lives dreaming, creating, connecting, and producing. Their dream home is the one where they live and they do not have to be the first to try something new. Their hero is the great inventor. With 26% calling themselves "citizens of the planet earth", they rank tied for second. To the Creators, the American Dream is all about the freedom to pursue their passions (50%, the highest of any tribe). They also rank number one in defining the Dream as "being my own person (39%) and "defining success on my own terms (31%). They are the second highest tribe in saying they are pursuing their own Dream. Two in five (40%) say the American Dream is alive and well and 45% wholeheartedly believe in it – the second highest.

CHAPTER 4

WE ARE ONE: TRIBAL BORDER CROSSINGS

We don't always get to meet our heroes, especially in adulthood, but I actually got to have dinner with my hero a few years ago at the Reform Club in London. I had been asked to join the advisory board of the AMAR Foundation, founded and led by the Baroness Emma Nicholson, a former member of the British House of Commons and now a member of the House of Lords. AMAR builds and operates clinics in war zones like Iraq, Yemen, and Lebanon for a mere fraction of the cost of big United Nations and Agency for International Development projects. Upon joining with Emma, I learned that a fellow advisor was the eminent historian Theodore Zeldin, a well-known expert on French and European financial history. He had written a book in the 1990s which had a profound impact on my thinking. Zeldin, a professor at Oxford University, wrote *An Intimate History of Humanity* , a fascinating series of vignettes about the development of our emotions and sensibilities across history and cultures. His fundamental theme argued that we humans may derive from specific communities but we are all the sum total of all peoples and cultures that have inhabited this planet for thousands of years. In short: we are many but we really are one.

This thinking has illuminated my work ever since I read the Zeldin book in 1995. And it has had a profound impact on my study of demographics and now tribes. Of course the eleven tribes are distinct and it is a powerful insight to see how we choose to be who we are and who we admire or follow or lead on the basis of common interests. At the same time that we look at those characteristics as markers that make us distinct from other tribes, my work has also revealed the prevalence of what I call "tribal border crossings" – i.e. areas of interest that are shared not only by members of other tribes but also by members of tribes who seemingly are very different to the point of hostility.

The value in understanding these border crossings is in the development of our skills in the art of communications, marketing, and leadership. I have written before many times on how Americans – particularly Millennials – have a well-honed bullshit barometer and are, at the same time, so distrustful of institutions that are supposed to be familiar and trustworthy. Without my getting into the entire story again on the breakdown of that trust, suffice it for me to say that those who lead institutions – church, state, non-governmental organizations, business – have lost the ability to communicate that trust. Instead, they opt to lead by segmenting when they could get much further (and actually produce more trust) it they sought to bind and heal differences. In short, if they could be more willing to find the border crossings and emphasize where we can agree as opposed to assuming that winning (or selling or saving souls, or appealing to donors) is an act of war, organizing just their loyal troops and mobilizing them alone. In short, we can have both the fruits of diversity and the understanding of people while they are acting within the context of the people with whom they are most comfortable, while at the same time we are seeking to aid them in building bridges and allowing to think and act in sync with others from other tribes. Why play up differences when so much more can be attained by heightening commonalities?

So we know that people cluster with their like-minded peers. We know that some have chosen to live in close proximity to those with whom they agree on life, politics, and culture. We now are seeing through my research that in the 21st Century, these clustering patterns are more and more transcending spatial and geographic limitations. People can cluster, bond, communicate, and act together without even leaving their homes. We also have significant tribal differences. The cynical Outsiders have little in common with the Go With the Flow. The Happy Hedonists are certainly not the God Squad or the Land of the Free, although maybe they are the children of them. The Adventurists and Self-Perfectionists do not see eye to eye on most things. This is what I call *tribal dissonance* – i.e. tribes that are radically different in many (even most) ways. It is the stuff of what young marketers and political consultants build the foundations of their careers upon. How best do we find our supporters, our brand loyal, our guys – and even more importantly , how do we reach them and exploit them? Sometimes this is reduced to the absurd. In 1981, before I established the polling business, I tried to run for the Democratic nomination for mayor of my hometown, Utica, NY. My job was a simple one: knock on doors of registered Democrats only and try to get a total of 1,200 signatures to qualify me for the ballot. Along the way, I of course met independents and Republicans and took time to chat, discuss potholes and noise abatement and runaway utility rate hikes – but fine, I was running to be their mayor, too. One evening I watched a good friend across the street as he went through the same process for a seat on the city council. Also running as a Democrat, Nick (not his real name) was obsessed with his Democratic file and avoided waving to non-Democrats sitting on their front porches or doing some gardening. Why? Because they were not Democrats and could not help him get on the ballot during that phase of the campaign. (Now we both lost but that is a whole other story for another time!)

But my view is that the obsession with targeting, segmentation, and micro-campaigns both politically and commercially is wrong, counter-productive and limiting. It is all about us not about them. In fact, at least in the world of politics, "they" and "them" are the enemies and need to be discouraged from going to the polls. In the worlds of marketing and communications, more efforts at finding common denominators will work well even as meta data is used to micro target. There are common values and emotional appeals that are essential to any kind of persuasion.

Tribes are loose today. Is anything really permanent these days? People have so many sources of information that they needn't be dependent upon tribal leaders for all of their information, their biases, and the definitions of their enemies. Sure, we lean on our tribes and get a lot of our identities from tribal members – but we are now more than ever free agents and capable of interacting and exchanging with others. As important as the tribes themselves are, their borders matter a lot, too, because that is where most people live. True, there's a hard core within every tribe, a group for whom, say, the "greenness of a product or its domestic content or a preacher's blessing is the absolute essential element. The rest of us, though, live with our right foot in one tribal zone and left foot in another, and those border straddling vary based on the product or service being offered. Clearly this provides a rich opportunity for marketing products and services that fill the crease between tribes and that cross over into adjoining tribal territories. In the words of market research Joe Plummer:" The neo-tribal framework as offered by Tribal Analytics is a fantastic way to integrate brand campaigns across touchpoints".

Thus I want to look at tribal identification as actually a bridge-building effort – born from segmentation – and not as an act of war or isolation. Let's first examine how the tribes in this book actually overlap. The eleven tribes differ in important ways from each other. They are distinct and need to be seen that way. But even seemingly divergent tribes have some interesting areas of convergence which can be most useful to advertisers, communicators, political strategists, and fundraisers. It is these **counter-intuitive border crossings** that offer a way to message to tribes that are very different on the surface but share some common points of interest. From the multiple phases of survey research, here is how the actual tribal identifications overlapped with each other. In other words, here is each tribe's members cross-identified with their "second-choice" and "third-choice" tribes.

BORDER CROSSINGS

TRIBE	CROSSOVER TRIBES
Go With the Flow	Land of the Free (21%), Dutifuls (15%), and Happy Hedonists (13%)
Happy Hedonists	Adventurists (18%), God Squad (13%)
God Squad	Dutifuls (28%), Land of the Free (22%), One True Path (15%)
Persistents	Land of the Free (33%), Dutifuls (21%), God Squad (16%)
Self-Perfectionists	Land of the Free (33%)
Adventurists	Land of the Free (22%), Happy Hedonists (14%), God Squad (13%)
Land of the Free	God Squad (24%), Dutifuls (21%), Persistents (15%), Creators (12%)
One True Path	God Squad (36%), Dutifuls (21%), Land of the Free (21%), Happy Hedonists (10%)
Outsiders	Hilarious (21%), Go With the Flow (14%), Land of the Free (14%)
Dutifuls	God Squad (29%), Land of the Free (20%)
Creators	(Land of the Free (36%), Persistents (16%)

So what are the common denominators that explain each of these? The Go With the Flow can have three distinct faces: one that appreciates the independence of the Land of the Free, another requires the stability and obedience to the rules of the Dutifuls, and still another that enjoys local sports with the Happy Hedonists. The key here is that there are in fact common denominators and messaging to the Go With Flow which can go well beyond the one-dimensional language of John Lennon's "turn off your mind, relax, and float downstream" to a more rounded appeal to freedom, independence, perseverance and even simple fun.

The Happy Hedonists are no doubt siblings -- though not twins -- of the Adventurists, but they have a saintly element to them as well – the 13% who relate to the God Squad. Thus, even materialists and tailgaters must go beyond Thursday night happy hours and Saturday night sins to be reminded that that they need a moral compass and a Supreme Being. And about one in four is the "free-spirited horse" portion of the Land of the Free. Imagine, in that sense, two tribes with a widely varied concept of freedom still capable of bonding.

The God Squad has an extended family that includes the Dutifuls, the Land of the Free, and the One True Path. Now clearly there is an ideological component to this relationship – social conservatism, old-time religion, traditional values. But there is also a bond that grows out of each tribe's need for stability and straight (no frills) answers to difficult questions.

The Persistents align closely with three very conservative tribes: Land of the Free (33%), Dutifuls (21%), and the God Squad (16%). All these strains are simply variations on the qualities that those who persevere need to survive and overcome – traditional values and the help of God.

Self-Perfectionists need the free-spirited independent streak of the Land of the Free (33%) but also the aloofness of the Outsiders (14%) – that sense that nothing and no one is quite good enough.

The Adventurists are quite a blend of unpredictable ingredients. First they crossover easily with the Land of the Free, the independence-loving, unfettered wanderlust side of their personalities. Of course, they are closely related to the Happy Hedonists, by age as well as just wanting to have some fun. And, then just like the Hedonists, there are the 13% who identify with the God Squad because, I suppose, after globetrotting, kayaking, rock climbing, and whitewater rafting, they have to at least think about the Lord's Day.

The Land of the Free are closely linked somewhat with their dues-paying counterparts in the God Squad (24%), the Dutifuls (21%) and the Persistents (15%). But the freest of the Free are the Creators – artists, entrepreneurs, movers and shakers.

The One True Path are a more secular version of the God Squad but 36% of them overlap in their identification. One in five (21% each) express an affinity with the Dutifuls and Land of the Free. They are all bedrock conservative – in fact each representing one of the fighting wings of today's Republican Party – the libertarian (LOF), the social conservative (God Squad), and the classical mainstream economic conservatives (OTP). But 10% overlap with the younger, more free-spirited Happy Hedonists.

The Outsiders are dark, brooding, and moody, but there are clearly elements that intersect with the GWF and the LOF – as in "don't tread one me, I'm busy being alone."

The Dutifuls, no surprise, close the loop with the God Squad (29%) and the LOF (20%). The three groups are all in line with each other.

Creators are on the move, energetic and entrepreneurial hence they strongly align with the LOF and the Persistents. Those engaged in starting up and developing an enterprise must be prepared to deal with struggle and adversity.

But how do those tasked to reach out to members of the tribes honestly make it work. How are the bridges actually built? In the final rounds of surveys, we asked a number of attitudinal and behavioral questions – especially the kind that reveal the inner core of feelings and values that say something about what people believe and cherish. On one hand, there were definite tribal distinctions. But, on the other hand, there were fascinating overlaps.

SHARED VALUES AND BEHAVIORS

TRIBES   ATTRIBUTES

We have learned what makes tribal members different but we also discovered things on which they agree. Even some key attributes that serve to define each tribe are shared by significant percentages of members of other – even very different – tribes. This next table shows some of these crossover attributes.

TRIBAL BORDER CROSSINGS: SHARED ATTRIBUTES

TRIBE	ATTRIBUTE (%)	CROSSOVER TRIBES (%)
Go With the Flow	Relaxed (28%)	Happy Hedonists (32%)
	Work in Progress (24%)	Happy Hedonists (32%)
		Persistents (29%)
		Creators (25%)
	Open-Minded (28%)	Happy Hedonists (24%)
		Adventurists (24%)
		Dutiful (24%)
Happy Hedonists	Open-Minded/Balanced (24%)	Go With the Flow (30%)
		Dutiful (24%)
God Squad	Blessed and Saved (49%)	Land of the Free (21%)
		One True Path (24%)
		Dutifuls (21%)
Persistents	Determined/Persistent/ Overcoming (32%)	Self-Perfectionists (23%)
		One True Path (23%)
		Creators (24%)
Adventurists	Work in Progress (24%)	Outsiders (33%)
		Persistents (29%)
		One True Path (23%)
Self-Perfectionists	Purposeful/Meaningful (20%)	One True Path (22%)
		Dutiful (23%)
		God Squad (21%)
Land of the Free	Freedom (24%)	Happy Hedonists (18%)
		Creators (15%)
		Adventurists (15%)
One True Path	Compassionate (25%)	Dutiful (21%)
		God Squad (24%)
		Go With the Flow (20%)
Outsiders	Rollercoaster (20%)	Happy Hedonists (14%)
		Self-Perfectionists (10%)
Dutiful	Hard Work (23%)	Self-Perfectionists (31%)
		Persistents (26%)
		Creators (22%)
Creators	Creative/Enriched (26%)	Happy Hedonists (14%)
		Self-Perfectionists (13%)

There is lots of potential for common ground.

We even see how some Happy Hedonists share some values and interests with the God Squad. As we saw above, the new-found passion for locally-produced food is not simply a liberal college-town phenomenon. Rather, every tribe (except the 40% of the Outsiders) includes a solid majority who pay close attention to the nutritional labels when they buy food. It is hardly a surprise that those most likely include the mainly liberal Happy Hedonists (70%), Creators (77%) and the conservative-leaning One True Path (71%). But the Dutifuls (68%), Go With the Flow (67%), Land of the Free (65%), Persistents (64%), the God Squad (61%) and the Adventurists (59%) are all paying close attention to what they eat. Among the leaders was the Self-Perfectionists at 76%. The quality and health of our diets has appeared to reach consensus support.

While not as high as the numbers of those who watch labels, other aspects of food health have influenced the tribes across the board. Locally-grown food (the "slow food" movement) started slow a number of years ago but has spread like wildfire across the nation. **Both the Creators (68%) and the One True Path (64%) top the tribes in paying close attention to local produce, but they are merely the first among equals in this category.** Majorities of the Land of the Free (60%), Happy Hedonists (57%), Self-Perfectionists (57%), Adventurists (56%), God Squad (56%), Go With the Flow (52%) and the Persistents (51%) also pay close attention – as does just under half of the Dutiful (48%). On a local level and in both restaurants and supermarkets, there is an opportunity to establish broad themes that speak to the many, while niche marketing can still focus on special targets. Again, only the Outsiders at 29% -- 70% who pay no attention at all – are so outside the box that the box isn't even in sight.

Just think back approximately 12-15 years ago when words like "sustainability", "scarce resources", and "climate change" were within the purview of only a very few people. Today, around half to two-thirds of every tribe tell us that they pay close attention to the "environmental safety" of the contents and production of the food they eat. The Adventurists (65%) and Creators lead (64%), but the top tier of concern includes the conservative-leaning One True Path (58%), the Self-Perfectionists (55%), the Persistents (52%), and the Go With the Flow (50%) – while just under a majority of Happy Hedonists (49%), the Outsiders (49%), the God Squad (46$), Land of the Free (45%) and the Dutiful (44%) pay close attention. There are certainly disagreements on the specifics of the causality of global warming, but a substantial number of Americans have caught on and do pay attention. This agreement should (and must) be the focus of the debate. This is a major cultural change and a good starting point for the conversation and policymaking on the issue.

The issue of the use of genetically-modified organisms (GMOs) in food production has dominated the food debate in Europe for decades but has just begun to be a focus of attention for Americans. It is clearly on the radar-screen of America's tribes. How many watch out for GMO use? The One True Path (51%), the Adventurists (49%) and the Creators (47%) top the list. But the other tribes range from a high of 41%-46% (Persistents, Self-Perfectionists 43%, God Squad 42%, and Outsiders 41%) to a low of 34%-39% (Land of the Free, Dutiful, Go With the Flow and Happy Hedonists). In just a few years the awareness of the use of GMOs has grown substantially. And this attentiveness cuts across demographics, ideologies, and tribes.

I personally do not enjoy shopping but I do like to see what is on the shelves, how it is merchandised, and how shoppers watch and weigh their decisions. I also like to guess at who is in the stores. Are they like me or are they different? We tend to think of "big box" stores as niches based on their brand, the brands and celebrities who are identified with them, and the demographics of their location. But I like to probe further and I love developing what I have been calling for years "retail politics" – i.e. just what are the politics and beliefs of those who prefer one store over the others. A regular Zogby Analytics survey question for years has been to ask "if there were only one store left for you to shop, which of the following would it be?" That is certainly one good way to get their favorite store – then crosstabulate that against political beliefs. From a super sample of about over 3400 American adults, here are each tribe's three favorite stores:

Go With the Flow	Target (26%)	JC Penney (15%)	Macy's (11%)
Happy Hedonists	Target (22%)	JC Penney (1%)	Macy's (13%)
God Squad	Target (23%)	Kohl's (17%)	Macy's (15%)
Persistents	Target (22%)	Macy's (15%)	Kohl's (14%)
Self-Perfectionists	Target (29%)	Macy's (15%)	Kohl's (12%)
Adventurists	Target (20%)	Kohl's (15%)	Macy's (11%)
Land of the Free	Target (28%)	Kohl's (14%)	Macy's (12%)
One True Path	Target (28%)	Kohl's (14%)	Macy's (12%)
Outsiders	Target (28%)	Macy's (16%)	Kohl's (15%)
Dutifuls	Target (23%)	Kohl's (17%)	Macy's (12%)
Creators	Target (22%)	Macy's (19%)	Kohl's (12%)

I also wanted to know which of the big box stores listed "least represented your values as a person":

Go With the Flow	Neiman Marcus (27%)	Bloomingdales (19%)
Happy Hedonists	Neiman Marcus (19%)	Filene's, Sears (11%)
God Squad	Neiman Marcus (25%)	Bloomingdales (17%)
Persistents	Neiman Marcus (25%)	Bloomingdales (16%)
Self-Perfectionists	Neiman Marcus (25%)	Bloomingdales, Kohl's (12%
Adventurists	Sears (26%)	Neiman Marcus (19%)
Land of the Free	Neiman Marcus (32%)	Bloomingdales (20%)
One True Path	Bloomingdales (17%)	Neiman Marcus (16%)
Outsiders	Sears (28%)	Neiman Marcus (25%)
Dutifuls	Neiman Marcus (34%)	Bloomingdales (21%)
Creators	Neiman Marcus (26%)	Bloomingdales (13%)

What do we learn from this exercise? First and foremost is that Target is a survivor. Even thought it has suffered a major cyber attack, it seems to have weathered it in the public mind. Much of its reputation is based on longtime presence, its outreach to rural America before anyone else did, and the quality of appliances and hardware. But there is much more. We asked which store would you want to stay around if you got to choose any one. Target is now the comfortable old shoe and the favorite lounging around shirt. It is a part of us and its appeal is across the board: it is the top pick by nine of the eleven tribes and comes in second place among the other two. It comes out on top among all tribes.

Generally in a strong place are Macy's, JC Penney and Kohl's. Macy's means New York City, *The Miracle On 34th Street,* and upper-scale without being haughty. And like Sears it is a survivor. JC Penney appears to have turned itself around after a disastrous change in leadership and elimination of a number of popular traditions. And Kohl's is now the second largest department store by retails sales in the United States, just after Macy's makeover that totally misread the minds, hearts, and coupon-scissors of its customers.

Members of the tribes also have reached consensus on which stores just don't represent who they really are as people. By origin and branding, Neiman Marcus and Bloomingdales have always been defined as luxury stores, upscale and expensive. One would have thought they would be aspirational as well – if you could only have just one store left wouldn't you prefer the store of your dreams? The best, the most high quality name brands, the stuff of 1930's and 1940s movie legends. I have already answered that question in my 2008 *The Way We'll Be: The Zogby Report on the Transformation of the American Dream* where I present and explain data from over a decade of Zogby polls suggesting that Americans are eschewing luxury shopping for affordable necessities and simpler pleasures. The tables above further confirm the cultural presence of what I have referred to as a growing sense of "secular spiritualism". In this case, Neiman Marcus appears as either the least or second least likely to represent the values of individual tribal members in all 11 tribes, while Bloomingdales appears in first of second place 10 of 11 cases. But again, there is agreement among the lower scale Land of the Free, God Squad and Persistents as well as among the hipper Creators, Happy Hedonists and Adventurists.

In the same vein, "America loves Dunkin". By reputation, Dunkin Donuts sells donuts and coffee and Starbucks sells an experience -- the formal practical, the latter aspirational. In our surveys, coffee outsells the ambience and fantasy. What is particularly stunning, however, is the degree to which all of the tribes prefer Dunkin Donuts. Some margins are tighter – e.g. Creators favor Dunkin Donuts 37% to 32% and Adventurists 44% to 36% -- but the margins are wider among a wide spectrum of tribes including the Happy Hedonists who favor Dunkin over Starbucks 54% to 28%, just like the God Squad (46%-27%), Persistents (48%-29%), Self-Perfectionists (44%-32%), Land of the Free (52%-22%), One True Path (42%-26%), Outsiders (44%-27%) and Dutifuls (48%-23%). When we ask "how about if we settle our differences over a cup of coffee? " Polling shows it can work. At Dunkin Donuts.

I would never have expected gun ownership to provide possible bonding moments. This table shows the responses to the very simple question, "do you personally own a gun or other firearm?"

	GWF	HH	GOD	PER	SP	ADV	LOF	OTP	OUT	DUTI	CRE
YES	30	40	31	32	22	29	33	27	18	27	20
NO	62	57	64	64	72	63	59	69	77	69	69

A majority of each tribe does not possess a firearm and that may be for a variety of reasons. The key here is the considerable degree of sameness on percentages among the tribes who do. Now, for sure, the Land of the Free would top the list and the God Squad is right up there as well. But 40% of the Happy Hedonists? Thirty percent of the tribe that seeks balance – the Go With the Flow? Even 20% of the Creators? Perhaps the good news here is that only 18% of the misanthropic Outsiders carry heat and 77% do not. The real point is that guns are an issue that not only split us as a people, but at times drive us into a frenzy. To date, those who possess have been more consistently passionate about their gun rights than the gun control activists who seem only to come out after a horrible mass killing. Nonetheless, this is enough to show me that appeals to both sides must be done with meta arguments rather than micro-targeting.

Even the issue of gay marriage. Our surveys posed the following statements about the definition of marriage :

Which statement comes closer to your opinion - A or B?

Statement A: *Marriage is a solemn vow between only a man and a woman. States do not have the authority to legally recognize benefits of marriage between anyone else.*

Statement B: *Marriage is a solemn vow between two adults regardless of their sexual orientation and married partners should be fully protected by the law and the benefits of marriage should be legally recognized.*

	GWF	HH	GOD	PER	SP	ADV	LOF	OTP	OUT	DUTI	CRE
MAN/ WOMAN	40	37	71	44	44	36	55	57	40	50	26
GAY MARRIAGE	41	52	18	45	44	51	33	33	47	37	54

Certainly this issue is divisive. The more liberal tribes – Happy Hedonists, Creators, and Adventurists – are predictable in their responses – as are the more conservative ones (God Squad, Land of the Free and One True Path, and Dutifuls). More significant to me is the middle ground – the

Go With the Flow, Persistents, Self-Perfectionists, and Outsiders who are evenly split. But even on the definition of gay marriage, there are still one in three of the Land of the Free, Dutifuls and One True who agree with protection of gay couples under the law.

News of the impact of hard-blocking and hard-tackling in the game of football has dominated both the sports and regular news media during the past year. The National Football League has had to establish a compensation fund for those former professionals who claim brain or other neurological injuries as well as set up new guidelines for equipment and rules for how the game should be played. A few high profile players have announced they are quitting professional football for fear of destroying the quality of their later life and many high profile newsmakers and celebrities (including the President of the United States) have suggested that they would not let their sons play football. Even with all of that, solid majorities of every tribe agree that they would have no problem letting their sons play the game.

Would you let your son play football?"

	GWF	HH	GOD	PER	SP	ADV	LOF	OTP	OUT	DUTI	CRE
YES	62	70	64	60	62	71	67	59	66	64	61
NO	20	19	19	20	20	16	19	22	19	18	15

Just look at those numbers.

The game's future has not been hurt at all it would seem. And it looks like football is held favorably across the board. So the same people who look carefully at food labels and want their food produced locally are not bothered by any health concerns related to the

game of football. God, Country, Food, and Football – they all reign supreme.

Speaking of God. I have asked the question many times in the past just how Americans define God. Here is the question:

Which statement comes closer to your opinion - A or B?

Statement A *defines God as all powerful and ever present in our lives. He is the Creator, the God of love, and he governs all things.*

Statement B *says that God is the Watchmaker who is the Creator and then, like the watchmaker, sets things in motion to be governed by the laws of nature and laws of man.*

	GWF	HH	GOD	PER	SP	ADV	LOF	OTP	OUT	DUTI	CRE
CREATOR	50	48	81	54	55	45	58	61	42	54	40
WATCHMAKER	20	28	11	28	25	25	22	19	23	25	23

God the Creator wins the match and by huge margins. Too bad there are so many foolish fights about God when so many Americans seem to believe in the same thing. While there are indeed differing levels of agreement on God the Creator, fact is that this characterization leads approximately two to one among all tribes – higher among the more conservative tribes, of course. But the God the Watchmaker belief has about the same level of support among ten of the eleven tribes. Even though it is a concept that drove the Enlightenment era – from which the concept of a free United States of America was born – the notion is only adhered to by about one in four Americans.

There is surprising agreement among the tribes about which leading celebrities are their favorites. I presented a list of major box office stars – one list of men, one of women – and asked who was their favorite. In addition to fame I tried to be sure that each name represented a unique persona – a value, a certain character, something special – lest there be any confusion. Here is the list and the scores per tribe:

FAVORITE ACTOR	GWF	HH	GOD	PER	SP	ADV	LOF	OTP	OUT	DUTI	CRE
Tom Hanks	25	22	15	19	17	20	16	17	22	22	17
Denzel Washington	22	28	23	20	19	19	16	19	11	17	13
Johnny Depp	13	18	9	14	24	18	11	12	23	12	19
John Wayne	6	2	12	7	4	6	15	11	6	9	4
Clint Eastwood	10	9	15	17	10	13	20	11	10	16	11
Brad Pitt	6	5	4	3	6	4	4	6	2	4	7
Ryan Gosling	3	4	4	4	3	6	2	5	3	3	5
Shia Laboeuf	1	2	2	2	1	1	-	1	12	1	-

FAVORITE ACTRESS	GWF	HH	GOD	PER	SP	ADV	LOF	OTP	OUT	DUTI	CRE
Jennifer Lawrence	17	24	7	8	12	13	10	6	14	9	13
Julia Roberts	15	19	15	12	9	11	13	15	9	15	10
Sandra Bullock	24	21	28	32	25	34	30	30	23	30	22
Kathy Bates	4	5	5	6	9	3	4	6	10	5	4
Angelina Jolie	10	9	10	6	14	12	8	10	11	7	14
Meryl Streep	10	7	12	15	16	9	13	11	13	14	11
Kristen Stewart	2	1	1	1	1	1	1	1	-	1	1

Tom Hanks – versatile, real, everyman, patriotic, non-controversial, and scandal-free – and Sandra Bullock – all of the above, as well as America's

Special Sweetheart – dominate the list. Bullock leads among all but one tribe (Happy Hedonists who choose one of the youngest actresses on the list), while Hanks leads among most although he faces a serious challenge from Denzel Washington. Interestingly, Denzel does best among the Happy Hedonists, God Squad, the Persistents, and the One True Path – each with a substantial percentage of African American members. But there is more. All three actors share those very same characteristics listed next to Hanks. They are authentic, a quality that is dominant in today's America and one that promises to challenge (even threaten) the image of Hollywood as Tinseltown. On the other hand, Johnny Depp posts especially good support among the Happy Hedonists, Self-Perfectionists, the Outsiders, and the Creators – especially since those tribal names alone define the actor's own image. He is an "actor's actor", risk-taking, creative, and bounces back even after serious box office setbacks. Clint Eastwood is dominant among the Land of the Free, the Dutifuls, the Persistents, and the God Squad, though he does reasonably well across the board. And the Duke (John Wayne) seems all but forgotten among Happy Hedonists, Creators, and Self-Perfectionists, while his best numbers come from the most conservative tribes.

Among actresses, Jennifer Lawrence is not only hot and on the rise among younger actresses, she also plays a variety of roles that transcend being typecast or exploited. Like Sandra Bullock, she appears to be a very nice young woman. After Bullock and Lawrence, we see Julia Roberts' support similar across the board, Meryl Streep more preferred by older and more conservative groups, and Angelina Jolie receives a bump from the Creators – though her support is within a few points from high to low among the tribes. The Outsiders and the Self-Perfectionists like Kathy Bates more than any other tribe.

But it seems that nice guys and nice gals no longer finish last and the tribes agree.

On the other hand, the vital takeaway from our list of favorite "reality stars" is that the consensus point is "no one and not sure". So while Kim Kardashian tops the list, followed by Tyra Banks, Simon Cowell, Honey Boo Boo, and Heidi Klum, the winner of the sweepstakes is (allow me to say personally) nobody. This category scores in a range from a low of 32% to a high of 44%.

We also offered a list of bona fide heroic figures from American history and asked which one was their favorite American hero.

FAVORITE HERO FROM AMERICAN HISTORY	GWF	HH	GOD	PER	SP	ADV	LOF	OTP	OUT	DUTI	CRE
Thomas Jefferson	16	17	6	10	10	9	10	3	7	9	20
Abraham Lincoln	25	25	28	23	17	24	24	30	27	27	20
Teddy Roosevelt	5	5	5	7	4	6	6	3	2	5	7
Franklin Roosevelt	7	9	4	7	6	4	6	6	6	5	5
John F. Kennedy	10	11	13	12	15	16	12	15	15	13	15
Ronald Reagan	6	5	16	11	12	10	20	13	7	14	10
Martin Luther King	17	17	17	16	21	17	10	15	11	13	15
Cesar Chavez	1	1	1	1	1	1	-	2	2	1	1

Honest Abe just doesn't go out of fashion. Regardless that he was only a one-term Congressman who ascended to the Presidency, a man who did precious little rail-splitting, was a corporate attorney for the Illinois Railroad and making a good buck at it, and as President suspended civil liberties to organize a Union victory. **The legend of Lincoln remains intact.** He was our Everyman President and outsmarted and dumbfounded his arrogant "team of rivals" time and time again. His Emancipation Proclamation did not really – practically speaking – free one single slave but it set off what was tantamount to a General Strike throughout the Confederacy that strangled the Southern economy. He suffered from depression and his wife was bipolar but his shortened life was a triumph and for that Americans love him. Those are pretty impressive numbers across the board.

Reverend Martin Luther King, Jr. is perhaps not only our greatest African American. He is probably our greatest American – he fought a domestic war, risked and gave up his own life, and provided the conscience of the nation at a time when the violation of its most cherished values was being exposed to a the rest of the world. Dr. King mastered the art of speaking not only to his own supporters but to a nation of mainstream television viewers. This was during the Cold War, a simpler world of Us (the Good) vs. Them (the Evil) and King helped to open a sore wound that led to positive legislative and attitudinal change. His numbers as a hero reflect it. While only 10% of the Land of the Free lists him as their hero, this is still a significant percentage from an older, very conservative, and very white tribe.

Thomas Jefferson is also revered but not quite as much among the God Squad, the Dutiful, and the One True Path on the right or the Creators and Adventurists on the left. But his support is still impressive for someone who died in 1825. What is interesting to me is the battle between the legacies of Presidents John F. Kennedy and Ronald Reagan – the youngest and the oldest elected presidents. They seem to not only have equal support overall but have strong crossover support as well. Thus the God Squad, the Persistents, the Self-Perfectionists, the One True Path, the Dutifuls, and the Creators see them both as heroes.

There are several other areas where the tribes converge. When we asked which from a list of stars and celebrities the respondents would most likely believe an endorsement from, the top response among each tribe was "a family member". While 16% of the Happy Hedonists (16%) and the Go With the Flow (13%) were more likely than any other tribe to believe an endorsement from a Hollywood star, and another 10% of Happy Hedonists would believe a "TV reality star", no one else gave that type of star double digits and no tribe scored in the double digits for the Hollywood star, TV reality start, NBA, NFL or MLB players, or even a teacher. The 37% of Happy Hedonists who would believe an endorsement from a family member was the lowest in that offering, while the other tribes ranged from a low of 43%-44% (Go With the Flow and Outsiders) to a high of 62%-65% (The Persistents and the Dutifuls). So much is made of celebrity endorsements and people are more influenced by them than they let on in surveys, but it is also very true that key influencers in our lives are actually family members and influencers among our peers – notably members of our tribes.

Significant numbers of every tribe use Facebook at least a few times a week.

Use of Facebook At Least A Few Times Per Week

	GWF	HH	GOD	PER	SP	ADV	LOF	OTP	OUT	DUTI	CRE
YES	75	83	63	68	76	78	65	70	65	66	68

Look especially at the numbers of Land of the Free and God Squad. This is the new town hall, village square, family reunion, tribal pow-wow. Facebook cuts across all tribes and it provides a platform for ideas, recipes, political rants, dialogue, confessional, expressions of support and sympathy, pictures of grandchildren and newborns, and the all-important "I am eating a baloney sandwich."

Twitter has become a very important meeting ground for all of the tribes. While not as impressive as Facebook, Twitter has followers and users across the board as well.

Use of Twitter At Least A Few Times Per Week

	GWF	HH	GOD	PER	SP	ADV	LOF	OTP	OUT	DUTI	CRE
YES	35	47	23	20	35	22	17	23	31	13	21

Okay, it is not for everyone, but there are sufficient numbers for establishing common messages and common ground.

The same goes for Instagram.

Use of Instragram At Least A Few Times Per Week

	GWF	HH	GOD	PER	SP	ADV	LOF	OTP	OUT	DUTI	CRE
YES	25	42	16	17	29	25	12	18	20	10	17

The Happy Hedonists are far out ahead on Instagram but this is still relatively new and probably where Facebook was just a few years ago.

When it comes to giving to charities, there were key common denominators among all of the tribes. Chief among the factors for giving was if the organization "benefits kids". A range of 39% -47% cited this factor as the major one in their decision. And a range of 39%-55% noted that they needed to be certain that their contribution actually went to "help those in need". And 30%-46% demanded "financial accountability/know where the money donated goes" as the top priority. This is a fair amount of agreement across the board.

I believe we spend too much time assessing branding and advertising, wondering which specific groups are being targeted than we try to step back and see universal themes that can have a wider appeal to more people. Some brands have become iconic because their slogans reflect a universality in their message. In other words the brand captures not just a "generation" or a demographic", but a universal value, an aspiration for a better life, a real spoken or unspoken need, something in the pit of our bellies that needs to be addressed. For example, the famous Marlboro Man was popular worldwide whether or not it got people to smoke more cigarettes. It actually did, but more than that, the man on the horse represented the free and rugged individual, unfettered by convention or institutions, just a man on a horse alone with nature. That image was something that people could identify with in the United States, Romania, and Kazakhstan. It was truly universal. So too was Coca Cola's image of global unity – "I want to teach the world to sing in perfect harmony." And, of course, two year olds worldwide can identify the Golden Arches before they can complete a spoken sentence.

We posed a long list of varied messages over the past few decades and asked our respondents to identify the two that best described who they are. The next table refers to the top four selections:

Advertising Slogans That Best Describe Who You Are

	GWF	HH	GOD	PER	SP	ADV	LOF	OTP	OUT	DUTI	CRE
Nike: 'Just do it'	38	39	20	22	25	30	20	19	23	18	24
State Farm: 'Like a good neighbor, State Farm is there'	15	25	17	16	15	15	18	16	18	11	14
Coca Cola: 'Make it real'	14	18	12	15	14	10	12	15	18	11	14
Apple: 'Think outside the box'	14	16	10	17	13	19	14	13	10	12	23

While clearly some themes are more popular with some tribes than others, there is still either uniform support or a relatively small range between highest and lowest acceptability among the tribes. Thus, Nike's "Just Do It" truly captures the Happy Hedonists, Go With the Flow, Adventurists and Self-Perfectionists more – but there is still good support among even the God Squad, One True Path, Land of the Free and Creatives and Outsiders. It is enough to suggest that this slogan drives not only the fitness surge and whole foods craze as well as the entrepreneurial passion in the United States, but also fuels the Arab Spring, the Mobile Technology Boom in Africa and Asia, aging Boomers attending a Carlos Santana concert, and the Caribbean cruise. It is ageless, timeless, and belongs to everyone with a spirit. At the same time, with the possible exception of our Outsiders and Creators – who need time alone to think – the State Farm slogan ("Like a Good Neighbor State Farm is There") speaks to (almost) everyone's need to be a part of a community of caring. It is the communitarian sensibility we all need. Whether we are close or far – both geographically or otherwise – from our neighbors, we all want to know someone is there to help when we need it. And we shouldn't be fooled by the news stories of people just standing by and letting horrors take place before their very eyes. The Truth is that there are so many major and minor acts of heroism and good neighbor assistance that are too many to count.

Coca Cola's "Make it Real" is the global *cri de couer* for authenticity. It is behind the shopping trend of buying what feels comfortable not sexy and the "real woman" movement sponsored by Dove, by the growing rejection of plastic surgery and the move by young female stars to not be airbrushed, by the rejection of political campaigns and by the refusal to go to church. Worldwide, it is the rejection of regimes either peacefully or not so peacefully.

And Apple's ("Think Outside the Box") speaks to the burgeoning creative and entrepreneurial instinct. As Princeton's Alan Blinder has noted, today's twentysomethings will have had four gigs by the age of 30 and ten by the age of 40. We need to create our own gigs, to dream, to constantly be repackaging ourselves to make ourselves more marketable as we move from town to town, technology to technology, and gig to gig. Thinking outside the box is today's Marlboro Man on a horse.

Perhaps the most successful example of niche marketing and the role model for others that follow is the successful Presidential campaign of young Senator Barack Obama in 2008. Everything from identifying and nurturing donors to targeting messages to individuals was planned and executed perfectly – and again in 2012. But it also needs to be remembered that this was an adjunct to the meta-message of hope, change, a new direction, and a new demographic that combined to make this perfect so appealing to a majority of voters.

CHAPTER 5

TRIBAL APPLICATIONS IN THE REAL WORLD

As I have noted above in the Introduction, multiple research techniques have been used over the years to connect characteristics of people to consumer decision-making and leadership skills and potential. The very same is true in the world of political campaigns. The most basic of them is simple demographics, but simple demographics don't tell us how people adjust to change. Psychographic profiling takes polling a quantum leap forward. But does it tell us anything about living in a world of chaos and how we structure and find meaning in our lives? The fact is we opinion researchers too often spend too much of our time within our own four walls, reducing our data to simplistic common denominators. To find out best how people are adjusting and surviving the disorder in their lives, it works best for us to do what we do best: ask them what they are asking about themselves and how they are dealing with the change.

That is the great strength of Tribal Analytics. It doesn't rely on tricks; it gets beyond the surface texture of people's lives. It is built on self-identity – the fundamental questions that determine everything from consumption choices to presidential ballots. In the end, it is not about just achieving a transaction – it is about the kind of in-depth understanding that builds relationships. Get the relationships right and transactions follow, and much more.

According to futurist Watts Wacker, one of the biggest trends to pay attention to in the short run is that while consuming is never going to go away, consuming as the defining criteria for individuals is. But Wacker is wrong on this. Basing our understanding of people mainly on what they consume is like building a sandcastle. Instead, Tribal Analytics speaks to the fact that philosophical or attitudinal spaces vs. physical things and places are the defining criteria for individuals today. So when you are at a party you ask "What is the most important event that has happened in your life?" "What are the most important factors in how you choose your friends?" and "What is your motto that guides your life?" According to Dayna Dion, former Cultural Strategist at Ogilvy & Mather, "I think it would be very beneficial for marketers to apply Tribal Analytics to brand identity communications strategy work." She continues:

> *Organizations often start defining and expressing their brand identities from the inside out. They look within, at their heritage and history, their unique attributes and benefits and their 'personality' traits. They ask their target audiences to share their perceptions of the brand relative to its competitors, and test different creative concepts and messages to determine what will motivate those target audiences to consider, try or buy. But they often fail to see their brands from the outside. They understand their brand's identity within a narrow and confined category landscape, but often lack a deeper understanding of their brand's identity within the broader cultural and tribal landscape that surrounds their categories.*

Tribal Analytics can help marketers understand not only who within their categories they want to attract to their brands, but who they do attract within our society's tribal landscape. Brands that understand their place within culture, and not just within their respective product or service categories, have a better shot of transcending their categories and establishing true cultural relevance. Marketers can also benefit from understanding the gap between who they want to attract to their brands and who they do attract. A brand targeting people who fit the Adventurists profile may in fact be attracting people who belong to an entirely different tribe, which of course carries messaging and media implications.

A few years ago when Dayna was still with Ogilvy, we did a "test run" where we incorporated many of Ogilvy's client brands and their competitors into the Tribal survey. At the time, we learned, among many things, that one of their prominent baby products was targeting "Go with the Flows" but was actually 'organically' attracting more Self-Perfectionists.

TARGET AUDIENCE PROFILE OR PERSONA DEVELOPMENT

In recent years, marketers have started behaving more like publishers than strictly advertisers. Content creation and curation are critical components of marketing strategies today, which makes audience understanding more important than ever. Tribal Analytics can enrich the target audience profiles or personas marketers develop to inspire their content strategies. It can provide a rich cultural "overlay" to the usual syndicated data and secondary insight sources that inform marketers' target audience profiles or personas. Traditional consumer segmentation work focuses on defining and profiling different audiences within a particular product or service category. It answers questions such as, "What defines and characterizes people who choose to stay at luxury hotels versus bed and breakfasts?" But it doesn't uncover the Tribes luxury hotel versus B&B travelers identify and "travel" through life with. Understanding travelers' tribes — the beliefs, philosophies and predispositions with which they travel through life — outside of the context of a hotel stay — could help hotel brands enrich their understanding of where the people they wish to attract "fit" within the fabric of our culture and heighten their cultural relevance, and this principle of course applies to brands in countless other product or service categories.

In an article written by Dayna for *REFRAME*, The Cross-Cultural Marketing and Communications Association's publication, she addresses the value of Tribal Analytics within the context of "Total Marketing":

> *'Total Market' entered the marketing lexicon with a bang as the buzz surrounding the lack of diversity and inclusivity in marketing reached a fever pitch. Marketers scrambled to adopt the approach before it had been formally defined to demonstrate their commitment to inclusive marketing that reflects the rapidly changing demographic makeup of American culture and speaks to a multitude of cultural groups in more authentic ways. Yet disasters abound as marketers struggle to put total market principles into practice and fail to distinguish between cultural relevance and cultural stereotyping. What lessons can we learn from the people on the forefront of cross-cultural marketing?*

How can we avoid alienating the audiences we're aiming to attract with a 'Total Market' approach? For starters, marketers can establish a process that begins versus ends with looking at cultural groups. "Total market can work if executed correctly, but oftentimes the default is the general market. Cultural insights are thrown in as sort of a secondary concern or afterthought and, when that happens, they're not really cultural insights. They tend to be stereotypical, shallow or static, said Katie Eng, Director of Strategic Planning at PACO Cross-Cultural Marketing. "You have to be very genuine in your desire to want to market cross-culturally and your process needs to start with understanding cultural groups and then looking for common threads across them or nuances between them."

This is precisely what Tribal Analytics does. It identifies cultural groups — not on the basis of demography, geography or ethnicity — but on the basis of life philosophies that transcend and cut across them. In this way, it allows marketers to speak to the 'Total Market' in a way that reflects its genuine makeup. It helps marketers avoid identifying common denominators among cultural groups based on ethnicity alone, and identity more relevant common denominators based on shared life philosophies, outlooks and values that transcend ethnic identities.

What needs to be underscored right now is that I have produced dominant generic tribes. New tribes can emerge in, and some can disappear from, the national landscape. And new tribes that are particularly useful to specific products and client bases will also emerge. The point is that Tribal Analytics is indeed a dynamic process and the prototype methodology is in place.

This is the way to find the tribes that matter most to you and a key to how to use the information. Importantly, Tribal Analytics is a client-specific, tailor-made process so the tribes discussed above are the generics culled from years of research. But below are some of the ways I would use this methodology.

TRIBAL ANALYTICS AND TARGETED SECTORS

In **health care**, I think of Daniel Pink, author of *A Whole New Mind*, who argues that health and medicine of the present and future are more holistic – the intersection of the mind, body, and soul. Tribal identification offers a path toward grasping the whole person above and beyond the presented in a patient history and diagnostic chart. This has serious implications for insurance companies and public health officers and providers. What are the habits and lifestyles that expose patients to risks of diseases? How can these be altered? Does a Happy Hedonist who wants to play too hard, an Adventurist who is here today but wants to be gone tomorrow, a Persistent who has the moral fortitude to survive, an Outsider who doesn't trust anybody, or a Dutiful who reveres all authority and is willing to take her medicine and advice – do these folks warrant a completely different and unique approach? I believe so.

All sorts of **jury selection** methods have been developed over the years. Some are very helpful and enable professional psychologists as well as brilliant jury selection observers to use real data to make decisions. But tribal loyalties, preconceived biases, and ethical choices can reveal prejudicial inclination and potential responses to the merits of cases, expert witnesses, attorney traits and arguments, and manufacturer culpabilities or innocence. Can a Go With the Flow be the leader prototype that attorneys are looking for to sway other jury members or be the loan voice of acquittal? Is a Land of the Free ready to convict a defendant on the first day? Will a member of the God Squad accept a plaintiff who has led an immoral life? Maybe, if a trial is in a rural area, is a trial team better off with a One True Path?

In the more and more competitive field of **higher education**, not too long ago it was apostasy to use the words "education" and "marketing" in the same sentence. Today, students demand more choice, more immediacy, and flexible career options. Higher education cannot afford to do it all via bricks and mortar and the expansion of professional staff. Higher education already collects lots of data but does not capture students' tribal loyalties, their aspirations, or their real interests. The same holds true with understanding faculty. Is salary the top concern or is the ability to travel, to be free to research, the opportunity to lead in their field or their interest? Is it best to pair students in housing or social groups according to regional and demographic characteristics or on the basis of tribal membership and perhaps tribal border crossings? College and university presidents must provide strategic direction, broader trend analysis, and the language of change. So can teachers and counselors actually benefit from knowing if a student tends to be a Self-Perfectionist who is goal-oriented but not necessarily likable? Or an Outsider who is just going to squander one opportunity after another? There will be the Go With the Flow who will go along to get along and the Dutiful who make sure assignments are done on time – but show little interest in leadership. But there are also the Creators who may not excel in the sciences and need more of an emphasis on developing their human sensitivities. Then too there also are faculty who may be Creators and long for time spent with the Dalai Lama while there are the Self-Perfectionists who will lead but cause a lot of suffering to others in the meantime.

When it comes to **career paths**, move over Myers-Briggs. Tribal Analytics presents a new tool to help fit individuals into the new world of work. Too often our understanding of career paths is steered by student aptitude, aspirations, and outmoded definitions of space and geography. And far too often we hear the cliché "there are lots of jobs but not enough people to fill them". But new jobs may require characteristics like sensitivity, empathy, abilities to interact with similarly-inclined or different kinds of people electronically and over long distances. Who are more inclined to fit in certain kinds of jobs or gigs as members of tribes or sharing borders with other tribes? If travel is a consideration – then there are Adventurists. Does a job require less on the side of people skills but more along the lines of self-confidence? There are Self-Perfectionists. What about concern for the environment and social justice but also the desire to be close to family and place of worship. Sounds like someone from the One True Path. Or a little glamour, lots of time alone, a caustic sense of humor and staring at a screen. Hey, Ms. Outsider, have I got an opportunity for you. Who are the ideal to work from home? Who can handle part-time work but still integrate with others via screen the best? Who is more adaptive to being relocated at a moments' notice or is a self-starter who is ready to take a plunge right away? These are tribal questions – and answers.

I speak a lot to leaders from **state and local government**. In addition to encouraging economic development, housing, infrastructure, and balancing limited budgets, state and local governments agonize about how best to maintain their creative class and young people. I have found that too many times public officials are asking the wrong questions. "How do we keep good people at home?" But I have wondered just what exactly is "home" in a world that has redefined space and geography. To some degree, what has been sewn on cushions for centuries is most applicable answering this question: "Home is where the heart is". Not necessarily where you pay your taxes. So does an employee of a local government or state agency have to physically live in that city? Does he or she have to live in a place to help it flourish? Why not consider distance-sharing employability, problem-solving via crowd-sourcing among citizens (i.e. those who love your city but may not live there any more)? If surgeons can assist or consult on heart surgery via a video-conference, why can't a local government or a state agency rely on consultants and employees and problem-solvers in the same way? Local governments fret too much on "keeping local talent", but "locals" can live anywhere and still serve "home". The key is in both utilizing untapped talent within boundaries and ex-pats who live afar. So what if a great employee in the housing department is a One True Path and chooses to follow her spouse to another job opportunity hundreds of miles away. Does she have to be lost? What if someone in the economic development agency is working on a major project and must leave either to care for an elderly parent or follow his spouse? Is he lost? What if they are merely Adventurists and enjoy mobility but have a commitment to where they used to live? What about a school budget vote that you know that "seniors" would object to – but now you know that there are God Squad and Land of the Free women who want only the best education and solid values for their grandchildren? Or Self-Perfectionists who can really crunch some mean numbers and win some good credit for their efforts?

Professional Associations/Trade Associations and Human Resources need to understand much more about their members, employees, and prospects. It isn't just Millennials who are patching together (and/or prefer) working at gigs. There are Creators who view a job as a way to fund their real love – writing, painting, making chocolates or soaps, or simply dreaming. There are the One True Path who need to fulfill the mission of Jesus, the Torah or the Koran and do God's work in their community. There are Self-Perfectionists who are ready to give their all if it means rewards, achievement , or any special notice to massage their egos. Or the Go With the Flow and Dutiful who simply want the job.

Fundraising for **not-for-profits** must follow a whole different model these days and well into the future. The competition is steep and pretty well gone is the era of the so-called "Pyramid" – i.e. raising 60%-80% from the huge major gifts. These days the message has to be targeted and the approach must be to go deep – instead of $10,000 from 35 people it has to be $35 from 1,000 people. What are the messages? For the God Squad it is promoting God's will, while for the One True Path it is the moral imperative and compassion. For Happy Hedonists it may be the cool thing to do, especially if it is done with friends. And for the Persistents it is a matter of recognizing that others have had to suffer and be redeemed. The point is that it is vital to find the tribal model and messages that fit because charities just no longer survive on worn out lists of major donors and anemic endowments.

If there is an industry that relies heavily on outmoded models it is **financial services**. Prospects are hunted down by age, referral, neighborhood, and community associations. Age cohorts are vital to understand in this field because generally they share worldviews that set them apart from other age cohorts. In broad terms, young people don't expect Social Security so they can be persuaded to save and invest, but many also want to travel and many understand that if they can find work, it may be a gig and not a job. There is little permanence, even if they are lucky to get a start. They are less susceptible to the "home-buying myth", especially when they are likely to be mobile and flexible. If one million Baby Boomers can expect to reach the age of 100, just wonder how many Generation Xers will reach that milestone in good health? Social Security and pensions will not be sufficient, and in good health they will have to and want to work anyway. The financial services industry has come up with assisted living insurance and savings set asides so that people can enjoy their Golden Years, but what about those who will still be living and healthy in the Diamond and Platinum Years? But this is about lifestyle, diet, exercise, good habits, outlook, and nurturing culture as much as it is about age. And more and more Americans – regardless of age or locale – care deeply about social investments that are consistent with the environment, the human rights of peoples abroad, and the protection of community jobs. So it seems that financial advisors need to be aware of the Outsiders in the midst as well as the wide variety of Happy Hedonists, the Dutiful, and the Persistents. There are indeed border crossings that can unite some segments of all these tribes, but I only see mainly a one-dimensional world of pitches coming from this profession thus far.

Truly **global companies** need to understand the changing employment market in all of its variability. No one understands this better than former IBM Chairman and CEO Sam Palmisano who coined and developed the term "the globally-integrated enterprise", by which he means the new multi-national corporation that recognizes that employees will be mobile and "7 and 24", located in clusters and integrated by distance networks. How best to build and nurture these networks and how best to find the prototypes of this new era worker? And do global companies big and small best move beyond grasping their employees' work-related connections toward creating positive outlets for charitable interests and activities? I think Outsiders are ruled out of this package and so too are probably Go With the Flow, Persistents, God Squad and Land of the Free. It sounds like the optimum targets are the Adventurists and Happy Hedonists for their wanderlust, desire for excitement, preference to travel, and flexibility -- along with the Self-Perfectionists, Creators, and One True Path because of potential opportunities to be imaginative, to lead, and to serve a broader purpose.

There are plenty of ideas on how to use Tribal Analytics in **retail marketing and advertising campaigns.** There is traditional media advertising, internet advertising, product placement, and "murketing" by organizing events large and small to appeal to influencers. But they all involve the creation of some buzz, i.e. getting people to listen about your product, talk about it with friends and family, and buy it. The world of advertising campaigns now represents the steady evolution, again in the words of premier market researcher Joe Plummer, into a

new mental model for marketing which involves aggregation and word-of-mouth instead of congregation/message interruption.

The latter involved seeking people in large groups (e.g. watching a television program, attending an event, driving on a major highway) and interrupting them with a branding message). Aggregation/ word-of-mouth means finding people with common interests, even at different places and times, and encouraging them to talk to each other.

I have taken a look at *Advertising Age's* "Top 15 Ads of the 21st Century" and have applied Tribal Analytics to a few to suggest how the process can work.

The Number 14 rated ad is for Chipotle, a two-minute video first aired during the 2012 Grammys. The video featured Willie Nelson singing a bit by Coldplay ("The Scientist") and was about a farmer changing his priorities from running a large agribusiness to focusing on "more sustainable and human practices". What was revolutionary was both the process – video too long for television and encouraging people not to purchase a sale but to identify with a value. Clicking got a viewer not a coupon but a chance to download the full video on iTunes and proceeds going to the Chipotle Cultivate Foundation – thus producing loyalty not directly from the cash register but to 21st century "food-industry issues". What Tribal Analytics shows us is that really all tribes pay attention closely to quality, environmentally-friendly, and healthy foods, have varying percentages (but still significant in numbers) of food-conscious consumers, and that consumers need not be one-dimensional coupon-oriented, fast- and processed-food shoppers. Healthy food is one of the ultimate border crossings.

The Number 8 is Apple's "Get a Mac" campaign, designed by TWBA. The series featured a nerdy/geeky "Bill Gates-type" character vs. a hip, more cosmopolitan "Steve Jobs-type" as characters. While the direct message was that Apple products (the Mac) are best equipped to help you deal with serious issues like security, viruses, rebooting and so on, the image was of the more appealing little guy conquering the Goliath. David, as we know, always wins that match up. The ads were entertaining and the overall takeaway was that Macs and Mac owners were clearly younger and cooler. The target tribes here would be the Happy Hedonists and Adventurists, of course, along with the Outsiders, Go With the Flow, and One True Path. The Outsiders are a focus because they need a reason to be seen as independent and set apart from the mainstream. Go With the Flow are are generally aligned with Happy Hedonists although they tend to be more self-sufficient. And the One True Path are mainly younger and hipper.

The Red Bull "Stratos" gambit came in at Number 5. This was not an advertising campaign. It was rather an event – the lead-up, the actual event, and the buzz that followed. It falls under the category of what journalist and author Rob Walker refers to as "murketing". The event was a record-setting parachute jump from 24 miles above the earth. It generated tons of earned media, millions of views well before the jump actually took place, live coverage, huge amount of buzz, and a large increase in Red Bull's U.S.'s sales. The messaging was the action and people continued talking about it well after it occurred. This has to be considered multi-tribal because it was clearly appealing to Adventurists, Happy Hedonists the Creators, and One True Path – all for obvious reasons. How could the Land of the Free and their Marlboro Man streak not go for it in a big way? Same too with the iconoclastic Outsiders.

The Self-Perfectionists had to just love the fact that it all focused on the daring action of one man. But it also probably got the God Squad and Dutifuls saying extra prayers.

Number 1 belonged to Dove's "Real Beauty" Campaign, designed by Ogilvy & Mather. This was not just billboards and television. It was a global cultural phenomenon that changed a conversation on what it means to be beautiful. It encompassed women who were young, middle aged, and older, of all shapes, sizes, and colors It came just at the same time that the fashion industry was forced to come to grips with models who were just too skinny as to be unhealthy. And it rose to the fore when both men and women were beginning to eschew fake symbols of both beauty and success. The timing for the message could not have been more perfect for the Millennial-led drive for authenticity. It won the support of the Girls Scouts of America and significant numbers of stars like singer Colbie Caillat and Oscar-winning actress Hillary Swank who demanded un-photo-shopped and non-makeup wearing photos. It has not only changed the conversation but changed a culture. It is easy to see how it has broad appeal to all tribes.

All of the sectors and campaigns noted above have relied on tons of market research. The Tribal Analytics approach can distill all of that into tens of pounds of market research by applying the methodology to tailor-make results per specific need and client.

SOME SUCCESSFUL "TRIBAL" ADVERTISING CAMPAIGNS

Some famous branding campaigns have special appeal for specific tribes more than others. For example, Coca Cola's "Make it Real" seems to be the most popular among the jaded outsiders and this group tops the tops when it comes to identification with Calgon's famous "Take Me Away" series. Both adds suggest a prime targeting among who are clearly dissatisfied with their lives and what they see around them.

On the flip side, Outsiders really want to be left alone – State Farm's "Like a Good Neighbor" is not for them at all.

Hebrew National's "We Answer to a Higher Authority" is not for everyone. Greatest appeal for this conservative religious slogan was among the God Squad (26%), followed by both the Land of the Free and Dutifuls (15% each) and the One True Path (13%). The other tribes, including Happy Hedonists, Adventurists, Go With the Flow, Creators, and Self-Perectionists were all in the 2%-4% range. It looks like a combination of "authority" and "religion" is toxic to these groups – both of whom are non-religious but more anti-institution. But I bet they all like the hot dogs.

L'Oreal's "Because I'm Worth It" seems to connect well with two very different tribes – the One True Path (12%) and the Outsiders (10%) but barely registers with anyone else. Other groups, as we have seen focus on authenticity but it is fascinating that a tribe that emphasizes its godliness can relate somehow with another tribe that is clearly waiting for Godot.

CHAPTER 6

TRIBAL ANALYTICS MEETS THE WORLD OF POLITICS

Successful political campaigns are about developing an organic mix of numerous variables – seasoned strategists, media creators and buyers; operations people who can handle the ground game; good polling and opposition research; issues that connect with target voters; building lists; brief messages that reflect the values of voters; and – of course – a good candidate. Ultimately, winning is partially about ensuring that all these pistons are up and running effectively, and also about knowing the target audience and communicating the right messages for each target in order to project the correct image. It is ultimately about winning and then being able to serve effectively after the victory. That means putting together coalitions for victory and for governance.

Tribal Analytics has an important role to play in this world of political campaigns. As I have noted above, an audience is more than just a collection of demographics or a congregation of party activists. Tribes are people with shared values, interests, priorities, and personal stories. Being able to profile this collection of individuals on the basis of how they see themselves is vital to any strategy. If we look at the most successful politicians of our era, we can see that some could instinctively – along with their good pollsters and handlers – divine their audience and speak to them on a personal basis. Richard Nixon's life was filled with resentments, slights, bitterness, and rejection. Who better to capture the frustrations of a Silent Majority of everyday Americans who felt they were lost in a country that was coming apart through no fault of their own? Who better to challenge the leadership elite than someone who felt deeply that this elite was in a longtime conspiracy to bring him down? Jimmy Carter was able to be the underdog ("Jimmy Who?") who through both a calm and unpretentious demeanor – especially in small group meetings one at a time in New Hampshire and Iowa – could promise to restore a sense that a politician could still tell the truth and not be above the lives of Americans. He was in 1976 the perfect anti-dote to the "imperial Presidency" of the Lyndon B. Johnson and Nixon era. Ronald Reagan was the master storyteller. Responding to stagfla-tion and international humiliation, Reagan spoke about greatness, hon-or, strength, and restoration – the "shining City upon a Hill". George H.W. Bush – the first compassionate conservative, saw a "kinder, gen-tler nation" and "a thousand points of light", and was able to transform the perception of patrician noblesse oblige into an image of a wise and solid leader. Bill Clinton could truly "feel your pain" in a nation filled with anger. He could also be smart and hip – a regular guy from a dys-functional family who genuinely knew what he was doing. And Barack Obama saw a nation badly in need of hope and optimism, as well as a changing demographic base. (I know, I skipped one President. Ran out of room! Sorry W.)

Tribal Analytics provides an efficient way to find the key tribes that will be supportive, identify either the small pockets of support among the larger tribes that will reject you or the ones that could lean your way, and determine how best to mold your message(s) to those tribes that can be persuaded.

First let's look at the generic tribes identified in this book and see where they stand on the political spectrum.

PARTY IDENTIFICATION BY TRIBE

TRIBE	★ DEMOCRAT	REPUBLICAN	★ INDEPENDENT
🐴 DEMOCRAT / LEAN DEMOCRAT			
Happy Hedonists	48	17	25
Go With the Flow	43	18	28
Adventurists	43	19	38
Creators	42	16	29
Persistents	40	27	26
Self-Perfectionists	37	26	36
Outsiders	34	22	26
One True Path	33	30	25
🐘 REPUBLICAN / LEAN REPUBLICAN			
God Squad	30	40	20
Land of the Free	30	37	27
Dutiful	33	34	33

POLITICAL IDEOLOGY BY TRIBE

TRIBE	★ LIBERAL	★ MODERATE	★ CONSERVATIVE
LIBERAL LEANING			
Outsiders	39	31	27
Happy Hedonists	36	40	23
MODERATE			
Self-Perfectionists	26	43	31
Adventurists	29	42	29
Go With the Flow	30	41	28
Creators	30	41	29
Persistents	23	40	38
CONSERVATIVE			
God Squad	11	30	59
Dutiful	19	36	45
Land of the Free	15	32	43
One True Path	19	38	43

WHO DID YOU VOTE FOR IN 2012?

TRIBE	★ BARACK OBAMA	★ MITT ROMNEY
🐴 OBAMA SUPPORTERS		
Happy Hedonists	78	22
Go With the Flow	75	23
Creators	69	28
Self-Perfectionists	57	40
Persistents	54	44
One True Path	50	46
Dutiful	50	48
🐘 ROMNEY SUPPORTERS		
God Squad	39	61
Land of the Free	40	57
Adventurists	46	48
Outsiders	45	47

POSITION ON ABORTION

TRIBE	PRO-LIFE	PRO-CHOICE
PRO-LIFE		
God Squad	60	26
One True Path	51	35
Land of the Free	49	39
Dutiful	48	40
PRO-CHOICE		
Happy Hedonists	29	60
Go With the Flow	26	53
Adventurists	35	53
Creators	31	49
Persistents	42	47
Self-Perfectionists	42	46
Outsiders	38	43

WHO BEST REPRESENTS THE VALUES OF YOUR AMERICA?

TRIBE	THE OBAMAS	THE PAULS
BARACK AND MICHELLE OBAMA		
Go With the Flow	52	20
Adventurists	50	30
Happy Hedonists	47	17
Creators	42	25
Persistents	37	24
Self-Perfectionists	34	23
RON AND RAND PAUL		
Land of the Free	19	41
God Squad	27	40
One True Path	26	36
Outsiders	25	33
Dutiful	25	30

Wow, there is a lot of grey area here. For those who think the political world is Black and White, Red and Blue, Right and Wrong—pay close attention to those five simple tables. Sure, there are the tribes that lean heavily Democrat and Republican – but there are tribal members who don't buy it. There are liberals,conservatives, and moderates, but there is plenty of uncertainty and disillusionment, so it looks like campaigns really matter. So take for example, the simple horse race question from 2012. The One True Path and the Dutiful are tribes that contain very few liberals and have solid pluralities of conservatives, yet they voted for Barack Obama over Mitt Romney. At the same time, two predominantly Democratic tribes – the Adventurists and Outsiders – voted for Romney over Obama.

I want to examine some of these nuances more closely. The Dutiful and Outsiders are a good place to start. The former leans conservative and pro-life, on the one hand, yet they still have nearly one in three who say they prefer the brand of America best represented by Ron and Rand Paul along with a solid one in three who choose to identify themselves as independents. So their values are certainly tilting on the conservative side but they are not in the bag for the Republicans.

As for the **Outsiders**, two in five call themselves liberal, but when we look at the Obamas vs Pauls table we find that one in three identify more with the Pauls than with the Obamas. This is not an uncommon confusion: libertarians calling themselves "liberal", perhaps more in the 19th century iteration of the term, i.e. free market, laissez-faire, "don't tread on me". Tribal identification is much more nuanced and I like that. In the world of campaigns, both candidates and their teams should be forced to work their way through the complexities of their constituents than face them as neat pre-packaged goods to be exploited.

At the same time, we see what on the surface looks like anomalies, but are relatively easy to explain. The Happy Hedonists are nearly three to one Democrat over Republican, thirteen points more likely to call them-selves liberal than conservative – yet a fairly high number own a gun, and about three in ten call themselves pro-life, and (as we saw above) they go to a place of worship more regularly than we might think.

The Go With the Flow are consistently liberal, Democrat, and love the Obama version of America – and they are the real problem for the GOP because they are a constant reminder that the party lacks balance. Every time, a Republican tosses red meat to Fox viewers and Rush Limbaugh and Sean Hannity listeners, this fundamentally modest and moderate tribe is quietly (and tastefully) turned off.

The same is true with the Adventurists. They lean Democrat over Republican, and they are much more likely to be moderate and pro-choice – and to favor the Obamas' portrait of America. But they also tilted, in the final analysis, toward Romney. Are they fit for the picking by the GOP?

I find the One True Path to be most interesting: younger, kinder and gentler evangelicals. They clearly tend to be conservative and pro-life – but they find the Pauls' America to be appealing and they voted for Obama in 2012. This is a group – the new face of Born Again Christians – that the GOP may be missing as it looks to establish a majority base. A lot of it could be that the GOP has boxed itself into a neo-conservative foreign policy (so contrary to a younger crowd of conservatives who only know failure when the United States gets too adventuresome), an anti-global warming position that flies in the face of a group that obviously is worried about the future of the planet, and an anti-immigration position that just does not fit in a tribe that includes a whole new wave of Hispanic evangelicals.

The Self-Perfectionists are moderate and as likely to be independent as they are to be Democrat. While they certainly lean toward the America of the Obamas over that of the Pauls, they are almost evenly split on abortion. Yet in 2012 they voted for the Democratic President's re-election. What is it about the current GOP that has not been able to convert these moderate independents?

Even three in ten of the very conservative Land of the Free and God Squad are Democrats and two in five of each voted for Obama, while – on the flip side – even one in four of the liberal and Democratic-leaning Go With the Flow consider themselves to be pro-life.

So how do strategists and candidates create bridges that can facilitate more cross-over voting? In other words, how do you win over enough members of tribes where there are pockets of potential to support for you campaign? Conventional strategies evolve around single themes that lend themselves to easy bumper stickers: Nixon, "The Silent Majority"; Carter, "I will never lie to you"; Reagan, "Are you better off than you were four years ago?"; Clinton, "Change"; Obama, "Hope". These may have worked well in a simple two-dimensional America -- one of Democrats vs Republicans and Red State vs Blue States, -- but are less likely to be effective today. Even if a candidate wins an election, how can he or she effectively govern? This is why I think it is better to understand people within their tribes, look for what pushes their buttons within that context, and then to find the border crossings (areas of intersection) to create winning and governing coalitions.

How would I do a national campaign these days? Let's say that both political parties have chosen their presidential nominees for 2020. And there is the proverbial billionaire candidate running for the nation's highest office. They are plotting out their general election campaigns.

THE DEMOCRATIC NOMINEE

If I lean Democrat, I know my party is pro-choice, pro-Second Amendment but favors some additional regulations, favors patriation of undocumented working immigrants, is inclusive on gay rights, will continue executive orders and promote legislation to reduce carbon emissions, and favors spending on infrastructure and rebuilding cities. Thus, we will assume continued strong support from Happy Hedonists, Go With the Flow , Creators, and Self-Perfectionists. **Persistents** can be counted upon to favor a party that polls show "better understands people like me" and is better suited "to represent the middle class".

But there are four tribes that present unique opportunities for the Democratic nominee that will need addressing: the Adventurists, One True Path, the Outsiders, and the Dutiful. For a tribe like the Adventurists, whose Democratic membership strongly outnumbers their Republican membership by a factor of 43% to 19%, who are clearly pro-choice, and who favor the values of the Obamas over those of the Pauls, why did it give a slight edge to Romney in 2012? This tribe needs an injection of optimism and hope. The Barack Obama of 2012 was coming off of a disappointing first term for Adventurists because this group had ridden an adventure of hope and change four years earlier. The good news for a Democrat is that 42% believes that "government can do good things" and more than any other tribe they strongly believe they are living the American Dream. They will not favor military intervention unless it is clearly a force for good and can be effective. Rather, as global citizens, they want to reach out to other peoples with softer American power.

The One True Path is clearly a conservative-leaning tribe, yet they are also very diverse – 32% are either Hispanic or African American. Thus they can be induced to favor the more inclusive policies of the Democrats, or at the very least eschew the harder line of exclusion of conservative Republicans. It is this new crop of mainly evangelical Christians who the GOP has to worry about. I assume that the 2012 GOP standard bearer, Mitt Romney, lost a few points with the One True Path by declaring in primary debates that he favored "self-deportation" of undocumented aliens. Above all, the One True Path prefers authenticity, compassion, and generosity.

The Outsiders are always a strange group. While they are considerably more likely to see themselves as Democrat, one in five (18%) are not even sure what to call themselves (higher than any other tribe), thus they are less likely to vote. They may be more liberal than conservative, but they are mainly nihilists, favor the Pauls' libertarian values over the government intervention of the Obamas, but still gave a slight edge to Obama in 2012. I think they are anti-person-in-charge, whoever it may be. They are driven by anger and rebelliousness. Only 5% are living the American Dream.

The **Dutifuls** provide a lesson for those candidates and political operatives who see things only in stark contrasts. Sure this tribe is conservative but they are generous and compassionate, favor choice on abortion, and thus tilted toward Obama in 2012. Above all, they are not mean. They simply are not mean.

THE REPUBLICAN NOMINEE

While there are only two tribes that are clearly in the bag for the GOP nominee – the God Squad and the Land of the Free – they are the two largest tribes. Mitt Romney won these tribes with huge margins in 2012, but they are not nearly sufficient alone to make the party competitive in 2020. So the GOP needs some serious crossover help and their biggest opportunities lie with members of the Dutiful, One True Path, and Adventurists.

The Dutifuls will respond to a conservative message on spending and a more modest position on pro-life. These are God-fearing people who have not lost faith in either God or government. They are deeply concerned about government debt but they tend to see the good in others and want to help. They tell us that they aspire to heroism in either war time or as "selfless missionaries". But appeals to the meaner side will fall on deaf ears. They are not so much anti-elite as they are disconnected from the world of elites. For the Dutiful, policies and candidates have to be especially family-friendly.

The One True Path are indeed a conservative tribe. But they are also the face of the new America. They too worry about government debt leading them "down the road to serfdom" but they will respond better to a more positive message. Their voting choice must be rooted in being hip, younger and adept at social media. They strongly dislike the excesses of the more exclusionary GOP and, as conservatives will respond to a more upbeat message that is aspirational and geared to help them succeed in their business and profession.

The Adventurists are deeply rooted in the American Dream. Anything that threatens their faith in things getting better for them can appeal to them. This is an optimistic and savvy group but they can be convinced that government spending to record debt levels is a nemesis to their fantasies of a better life. However, for them the old cliché is true to form: the candidate who smiles is the one who is more likely to get their attention.

THE INDEPENDENT

There seems to always be a third party waiting to be formed. There are plenty of jaded and disappointed folks out there who reject something or everything about both parties. Thus, there are members of the Dutiful who tend toward the conservative but really just want things to function smoothly, while there are Outsiders who get turned on by flame-throwing. The United States has had third parties and independent candidates that have represented some of the former (former moderate Republican Representative John Anderson in 1980) and a lot of the latter (Governor George Wallace in 1968, billionaire H. Ross Perot in 1992 and 1996, and consumer advocate Ralph Nader in 2000). Getting those who favor a more centrist, problem-solving, non-ideological approach together with angry populist rebels to form a critical mass and win elections has always been the major challenge. But let's take a look at how support can be built among certain tribes.

The campaign may start with a large dose of anger and rejectionism, but that cannot really sustain a long-term campaign. But in order to get started, I would focus on three tribes: the Land of the Free, the Outsiders, and the Adventurists – an eclectic coalition, no doubt. The Land of

the Free are of course very conservative, traditional, and homogeneous
. But they are a good source for the traditional "angry white male" base
that has nurtured Wallace, Perot, and the Tea Party over the years. For
them, the country is losing its core values ("God, Guns, and Gonads!")
and America, in their view, needs strength, clarity, straight talk, and a
restoration of our freedom. They see an America that is threatened by
terrorism, a moment of weakness as this nation retreats from its position
as the sole superpower, and a major show of strength against a world
that is slipping away from our grasp. They favor Republicans but not
wimpy ones. This country needs a man (preferably a white one who was
actually born here!) and a bottle of Viagra.

The Outsiders provide the filler. They are mad as hell about everything
and ready to fight – if you can get them out of their Mom's basement.
If you can't, they provide the poison pen that fuels the blogs, especially
the local **Topix** commentary in local media.

Now we need a major dose of resentment and youthful creativity. While
it appears to be very hard to reconcile the worldview of the Land of the
Free with the Adventurists, there are some intersecting values: the belief in
the American Dream and the profound fear that it might be slipping away.

To get to a majority I would look closely at the tribes that have less loyalty to either of the major parties and/or those who choose a more non-
ideological approach to issues. The Self-Perfectionists have the largest
percentage of moderates and second largest numbers of independents
(after the Adventurists). They also are less inclined toward nurturing
long term bonds.

CONCLUSION

I have learned so much from my three sons. It is now my youngest son's turn to be singled out. When Jeremy was a little boy we would walk together and he would look up into the sky and see cloud formations. He would tell me to look up in the sky and ask me what I saw. Frankly, I would see a cloud – but he would tell me that he saw a cowboy on a horse. And he was right. And that is why he has seamlessly transitioned from a successful career as a teacher to a research position in the expanding world of data analytics.

Jeremy is where he belongs and the practice of data analytics is the better for it. The capacity to produce data is unlimited and lots of it is being collected. But interpreting it is not merely an exercise in writing algorithms and generating good metrics. **Analytics requires the sensibility of the artist, the ability to understand people of the social scientist, and interpretive skills of the novelist, philosopher and poet.** It is very much a right brain activity and needs the adults who were once little kids who saw the cowboy on a horse in a simple cloud formation.

Thus the production of Tribal Analytics is about both good data and the ability to see new formations that make good sense.

I have lived and worked, built a successful business, and married and raised a wonderful family in the Mohawk Valley of Upstate New York. This is right in the heart of Iroquois country, among the most impressive and sophisticated nations among our early Native Americans. Actually they were six tribes with their own councils and economies, but, as the legend goes, to establish long-term peace and prosperity they needed to listen to the words of the prophet Hiawatha whose message from the Great Spirit was to establish a confederation of cooperation and collaboration to institutionalize peace among the tribes and to better prepare for any foreign onslaught. The Iroquois became the model for the 13 original states – the Articles of Confederation. Tribes are important and they are sources of comfort and security, but we are indeed interdependent and share a lot more than anything that divides us.

Americans are dividing themselves into communities of shared interests and these are vital for our well-being and spiritual comfort. But we need to listen to Hiawatha and the Great Spirit. We can celebrate our difference as long as we do not forget what holds us together. We are, as Professor Zeldin has remarkably pointed out, actually the sum total of everyone who has walked this Earth before us and who inhabit our world today.

I have found a process that helps identify the tribes we belong to on the basis of what is really important to us. While many segmentation studies do indeed begin with qualitative research designed to identify attributes and variables for quantitative segmentation, I believe what makes Tribal Analytics so unique is its philosophical vs. methodological starting point. My team and I did not start with an analysis of people as shoppers within a particular product or service category then build out from there. Rather we began with an analysis of people as human beings – "social animals" – and let them define for themselves the parameters of their social identities. **People told us how they categorize themselves in the world versus in a product category. From there, we could then**

illuminate how a person's perceived identity and place in the world drives their attitudes, beliefs, consumption and political behavior. In the process, we are not making any presumptions about the basis of identity – e.g. we are not presuming someone identifies with and makes choices in accordance with 18-24 year olds simply because they happen to fall within the 18-24 year old age range.

Of particular significance is that in Tribal Analytics we asked each respondent to go well beyond listing their most important attributes, their mission in life, their most cherished values – we actually asked them to name their own tribe.

This is just the beginning of the process. I especially like the fact that Tribal Analytics can be a real time process – prepared to capture changes, withering and burgeoning tribal identities, new responses to global and personal events. Thus, the major tribes I identify can fall by the wayside under different conditions. New tribes can spring up from nowhere. For example, the Outsiders were nowhere to be found in the first few rounds of surveys. There were indeed iconoclasts, radicals, the bitter and angry from the outset. At one point we found a group we referred to the as the Hilarious because their lives appeared to be one big joke. But subsequently rounds of surveys discovered that there were additional layers to their loneliness, rebelliousness, and boredom.

At the same time, we have to wonder what the future holds. What new tribes can emerge? Will we see a band of Neo-Hoarders emerge, a tribe devoted to surviving the "Next Big One" – i.e. stock market crash, the tsunami, or the next election? Or how about the "Not-For-Profits", a new wave of social entrepreneurs who both do good and do well in a zero-margin society? Or maybe "GIG-olos", the growing number of new independent workers who bounce, by necessity, from one project to the next in an economy that promises nothing long term? Who knows?

Are there other tribes out there? Just as we know and feel that there are other planets sustaining life somewhere out there, surely there are more and more tribes.

I hope this is not the end of the conversation about our tribes and tribal analytics. I hope it is just the beginning. I have developed a new approach to clustering and segmentations. Let the respondents tell us who they are and how they fit. This can be a great tool for fellow practitioners of the art of communication as well as for our fellow human beings in general. But finding the glue that holds our tribes together, speaks to our better angels, and captures both our aspirations and passions – that is ultimately what will make us big winners.

APPENDIX

FINDING THE TRIBES: THE METHODOLOGY OF TRIBAL ANALYTICS

Tribal analytics has been a seven year journey and it is far from over. The research for a new approach to segmentation began in 2009 at Zogby headquarters and was based on the need to find a way to establish new clusters that were less focused on demographics and more flexible to reflect a world that changes quite rapidly. Thus, after a few trials with Zogby online surveys we came up with the notion that new categories should be developed by survey respondents themselves and that Americans were reorganizing themselves into communities of shared interests --"neo-tribes" – i.e. arrangements based on similar attributes, common behaviors and aspirations, and the desire to base relationships with people who were more like "me" than family, age cohort, career interests and so on. The early surveys in 2009 and 2010 began with our assumptions as to possible clusters – God Squad, New Agers, Rule Breakers, Neo-Luddites, Global Mobiles, Secular Idolators, and so on. We developed four Likert Scale-type statements that we believed characterized each "tribe" and established an algorithm based on frequency and degree of agreement toward each. We found validation for 11 of these "neo-tribes" and cross-tabulated demographic, behavioral, political, and brand preference data against each. The results of this exercise were sufficient in our view to suggest that there could be tribal segments of the American population – and that there were distinctive differences and "border crossings" between and among neo-tribes. We spent those years exchanging intra-company memos designed at tweaking the survey instruments and the algorithms. We also authored two articles and a powerpoint to disseminate the ideas and test them in forums in both the U.S. (the Annual Conference of Campaigns and Elections Magazine and the Wharton School's "Conference on the Future of Advertising") overseas (the First Annual Prague International Advertising Festival). The idea was well-received but nowhere near ready for client marketing and adoption.

In the summer of 2011 we approached the Chicago-based Cultural Intelligence Division of Ogilvy & Mather and discovered a potential fit for our efforts on both sides. Ogilvy's team was working on establishing the broader cultural context for individual and group decisions. What is the influence of religion, literature, music, sports, family and more on how we think and decide? "Who am I?" and "Who are we?" Their research was taking them well beyond the narrow scope of defining consumers. Rather they were looking for a new (and bigger) approach to understanding people. The two teams conceptualized new methodologies and together came up with the idea of first probing key questions using an open-ended survey instrument.

During much of 2011 and 2012, following several attempts toward allowing survey respondents to establish their own tribes, we at Zogby Analytics presented our preliminary findings to the Ogilvy & Mather team and continued to work closely with them to refine the process, develop sharper survey instruments, and discuss how the information gleaned can be optimized by end-user clients. Our initial joint test came in the summer of 2012 when the two teams developed a battery of open-ended questions aimed at probing the most important values, friends, rules, brands, and ideas to Americans. The results and processes are presented as follows.

We employed a multi-stage series of surveys and analytics to derive America's "neo-tribes". Our mission is not only to more accurately represent where Americans categorize themselves today and to assist clients in finding, messaging, and delivering products and services to their key tribes – but also, to create a high-speed and flexible methodology that can capture "emerging tribes" and push aside "diminishing tribes". In two important ways Tribal Analytics segmentation is very different:

- It is dynamic and flexible enough to capture changes in patterns of people's lives and priorities

- It is bottom-up, not top-down, in its approach to segmentation in that it is derived solely from survey research with no pre-established hypotheses

Initially, as described above, the process was launched with three separate quantitative online surveys nationwide to test if the idea of tribes made any sense. In each survey we learned from declarative statements made to represent distinctive values and attributes that there were Americans who could clearly be categorized into groups that represented dominant values and worldviews. We also discovered higher correlations with certain types of behaviors. From these tests, we then found through cluster analysis that at times there was a clear pattern of "tribal border crossings" – whereby members of tribes were very distinct from each other but that there were intersections of agreement and other commonalities that allowed communicators to develop crossover messages. On the other hand, there were also patterns of "tribal dissonance", whereby differences were so profound and intense that these could actually resemble warring tribes of old.

Zogby Analytics and Ogilvy & Mather then collaborated in developing an open-ended survey instrument to begin the process of respondent-driven identification of neo-tribes. A random sampling online of 1019 adults nationwide answered the following types of questions:

- Life mission and meaning

- Personal motto that drives each person

- Most important events or life-changing moments

- Four or five qualities of the most important people to you

- One possession that people have that you would most like to have

- Name the one thing missing from your life that would make it complete

- The most important task you would like to complete before you die

- Factors in choosing friends

- The definition of success

- Naming of tribes

- Political ideology

- Presidential voting preferences

The 21-question open-ended survey also included quantifiable demographics and other political preferences. The Zogby team reviewed and categorized the tribes, attributes, and demographics that emerged. Initially, this process yielded 10 tribes by first packaging tribal names, consolidating them into manageable numbers, and correlating them with attributes, behaviors, and demographics. Following consultation with the Ogilvy & Mather team, we inverted the process and created tribal segments by focusing on attributes first. The results of the two processes were similar.

Following several meetings and conferences between the Zogby Analytics and Ogilvy & Mather teams through the fall of 2012, the next phase included a detailed survey to be employed January 2013. In this next phase, we used the attributes and tribal names derived from the July 2012 open-ended survey as the basis for formulating a 115-question closed-end survey instrument to be sampled among 1000 adults in the United States. Thus, instead of creating hypothetical segments then validating them, we validated the actual segments that emerged from the open-ended survey. The new survey included 13 key attributes that emerged, along with the tribal names we discovered in the open round. We were interested to find out how important and intense each attribute was to respondents both in terms of defining their lives and driving their decisions, as well as in choosing the people they most wanted to be with.

Additional questions revolved around self-image, aspirations for work and life, fantasies, shopping habits and preferences, politics and ideology. A total of 1009 adults completed this quantitative survey. Following the completion of field work we again proceeded to correlate tribal names with both the frequency and intensity of identification of attributes. Attributes included those derived from the open-ended survey that related to both self-identification and the most important in choosing fellow tribe members. From this point, we were able to consolidate almost every respondent into one of seven tribes.

After this exercise, we found seven preliminary "neo-tribes" that yielded sufficient numbers to warrant detailed profiling. Other neo-tribes existed but were insufficient in cell size to allow for statistically significant analysis. Any attempt to pursue the necessary broadening of the numbers of neo-tribes would have to wait until further surveys would be conducted that would broaden the pool of respondents.

LESSONS LEARNED FROM PHASE I

The Zogby team had thus far learned the following key points from Tribal Analytics;

1.   Beyond Demographics – we need new models of segmentation that represent the fullness and complexity of our lives. Members of each of the preliminary seven neo-tribes cut across demographic lines. While one demographic cohort or another may be dominant in each, demographic characteristics were by no means the key determining factors for membership in any of the tribes. Each of the tribes is truly eclectic by age, race, region, income, and educational level achieved -- and the areas of crossover from one tribe into another are not always (or even often) intuitive.

2. The Importance of Qualitative Research – it was the use of the first round of open-ended survey research that allowed us to find this new formation. It is a chief aspect why this approach is fresh and pioneering. The online random sampling method permits us to enable respondents to put their thoughts, reactions, feelings and other expressions into their own words. Over 1000 respondents to 21 open-ended questions provided us with a treasure trove of information and insights into how they defined their lives, aspirations, guideposts, friends, and most important events. This prevented us from the urge to develop a priori hypotheses and other kinds of speculation about who they really were. This provided the key to the development of Tribal Analytics. It also allowed us to obtain and analyze real words that provided insights into their emotions, priorities, and passions.

3. Dynamism – new sources of data collection on opinion research allow us to move beyond old methods of live telephone sampling. For tribal analytics, Zogby used its online survey methodology because it is accurate, fast, and capable of collecting significantly larger samples in a quick and efficient manner. (Facebook, Google Analytics, and other social media resources will allow us to do the same thing, although the online panel used by Zogby maintains the approach of random probability sampling. Even more significant, this is a nimble process. Previous methods of segmentation would take much longer, be much more costly, and quickly outlive their usefulness in today's world of fast-paced change. Our methodology allows us

to produce new tribes at the speed of light. The survey design and analysis allow for the emergence for the emergence of new tribes and the decline of others. Some tribes will conceivably live forever, but others may be ephemeral, momentarily reactive to specific conditions and events, or obsolete. The methodology employed is designed to be expeditious, cost-efficient, and up-to-the minute.

4. Client-Ready, Made-to-Order – the methodology is ready and appropriate for client application. Enough patterns have been established so that the survey questions that can serve as screeners can be streamlined to perhaps one third of the number. This accentuates the flexibility in the process. **While there is clearly a national model for Tribal Analytics and the Neo-Tribes, the methodology can be used for brand customers, shopper and employment profiles, and non-governmental organization donor profiles.**

ONWARD TO PHASE II

Obviously there was so much more work to do. We have shown that people can re-group on their own without "prompts" from professional researchers. We have demonstrated that there are some broad "tribes" that are unique, self-selected, and transcend simple demographics. We also know – and we think that this can have the most profound impact on how marketers, managers, and communicators conduct their business -- that there are areas where very different tribes actually do intersect with each other.

So what was mainly involved as we moved on to Phase II was simple: we need a larger sample. The simplest solution then is to use most of the same questions and demographics in two separate surveys of approximately 1000 American adults nationwide. Why separate samples? The first new sample is to determine if any new tribes have emerged. The second new sample is to allow us to then aggregate the results of three closed-ended surveys to create a "super-sample" of approximately 3000 adults. This would allow us to then create more tribes with more members and allow us to do our analysis more precisely.

We did not change anything at all regarding the sampling process but we decided to tweak the algorithm we used for analytics purposes. In the first round and in the first new sample, we employed a fairly rigid criterion to determine the correlation between tribal names and key attributes. In the aggregate samples, we decided we could loosen up a bit to allow for a less restrictive "membership" in tribes without in any way sacrificing the product of our work.

FIRST FOLLOW UP SAMPLE

Our next round of survey research came in 2013. Using the same algorithms, the premises behind the tribes and the tribes themselves held up. Employing strictly the same formula as before, six of the seven original tribes remained. The Land of the Free fell by the wayside, but a new tribe, the "One True Path" emerged.

Three major conclusions can be drawn from this round:

- Tribes can be based on attributes, not necessarily on behaviors, ideologies or demographics as in the past.

- The methodology, both sampling and survey instrument, is sensitive enough to capture both new and emerging tribes as well as those that are waning.

- More sampling is required to develop sufficiently-sized clusters to allow for smaller tribes to be analyzed.

Once the next round of surveys is completed and more tribes are formed, we would then need to develop a social media strategy. The neo-tribes are based on social formations that transcend geography and common physical space. So where do tribal members hang out?

But following this phase, we have actually been able to validate much of what we learned about the first seven tribes, add additional color to their descriptions, and add five new tribes.

PHASE III AND FINAL ROUNDS

In subsequent rounds, I was able to test the strength of the tribes by using 36 qualifying polling questions. What I mainly needed to find out was how important each of the defining tribal characteristics was to individual respondents both to themselves and in finding/maintaining their innermost circle of friends. I also was able to test the tribal names to see the correlation between tribal characteristics and names. Over the course of three individual samples of 1000 adults throughout 2013 and 2014, along with a super sample of over 2500 adults I found that the tribes stayed strong and viable.

The percentages of members stayed stable and I was then able to aggregate the tribes to further refine demographic, attitudinal and behavioral characteristics. By early 2015 we now had a supersample of 6400 respondents.

With the tribes now defined I am able to use the qualifying questions and a whole host of additional questions about values, positions on issues, ideological and religious identification, political leanings, and branding to flesh even more aspects of each tribe.

Tribal Analytics is not merely an identification of possible new tribes. It is a process that merges left-brain analytics with right-brain sensitivity to serve new packages of consumers and voters in a dynamic consumer- and voter-driven world. Thus, the quantitative rigor is present in the best practices of random sampling, social scientific data crunching, and clustering. But so too is the use of detailed survey instruments to probe the heart and soul of respondents to find best who they are, where they fit, and what drives their choices.

As a final note, tribal analytics is a flexible process. This methodology can be applied to customer lists, political party members, shopping intercept interviewees, attendees at a concert, or a myriad of targeted lists (Millennials, airline pilots, funeral directors, Major League Baseball fans, and so on).

ACKNOWLEDGEMENTS

I have been working on Tribal Analytics, as I have noted above, since 2009. There has been a lot of help all along the way.

Present and former staff at Zogby International (then Zogby Analytics) were instrumental in the formation of questions and the development of algorithms over the years. Karen Scott, Katy Schwalbe, Grace Ren, and Joe Mazloom provided much needed guidance and support. Dr. Zeljka Buturovic continues to be a great source of analytical, statistical, and social scientific skills for this project. Chad Bohnert and Marc Penz have worked strenuously to get both the methodology and meaning into suitable shape.

Since taking over the reins of Zogby Analytics, my son Jonathan Zogby has been a believer and guiding spirit into the potential of tribal analytics. He and my son, Jeremy Zogby, worked through the summer of 2011 painstakingly going through the tens of thousands of open-ended responses that led to the first real sketches of the 11 tribes. We are all richer for the experience because we actually let people speak for themselves and learned a tremendous amount about individual experiences and deeply held values as behavioral drivers.

Jeremy Katz was also an early believer and read through a number of iterations of this process and product. And he introduced me to Graceann Bennett and Dayna Dion of Ogilvy & Mather in Chicago who just got it from the outset and spent a good deal of time helping us develop it. I need to underscore especially the importance of Dayna who has been a true source of inspiration and boundless knowledge on the uses of cluster analysis and the understanding of human beings. Ryan Monroe, also of Ogilvy & Mather helped particularly with the use of key attributes as a source of packaging the new tribes.

Leah McDonald Hobaica has been responsible for the design and the whole look of this book. Doesn't it look great?

Author and editor Howard Means helped me formulate the original concept of the tribes. Howard has provided so much in terms of intellectual exchange. He is an original thinker of the first order.

I took advantage of numerous speaking events to test the response to tribal analytics and the new tribes. I note in particular, events in Prague (The First Annual International Advertising Festival 2010), Miami (The Food Marketing Institute, 2015), and Washington, DC (Campaigns and Elections Magazine 2012) as the events that provided me the comfort that I was on the right track. More recently, in October 2015, I presented it at the Madden Institute for Business at my alma mater, LeMoyne College and won rave reviews.

The manuscript was reviewed by some key people in the marketing and communicating industry.

I benefited greatly from my good friends Patricia Martin of Lit Lamp Communications and author of Ren Gen; Mark Steitz of TSD Communications; and Tom Edmonds of Tom Edmonds and Associations – consultants who are expertly involved in the practice of culture and communications.

As always, thanks to my wife Kathy and my son, Ben, our gifted lawyer, who are a perfect combination of Adventurers, Persistents, and Creators.

Thanks to all. Any shortcomings are my responsibility, of course.